THE
STUDENT
INDUCTION
HANDBOOK

THE STUDENT INDUCTION HANDBOOK

PRACTICAL
ACTIVITIES
FOR USE
WITH NEW
STUDENT
GROUPS

TOM BOURNER · JOYCE BARLOW

KOGAN PAGE

First published in 1991

Kogan Page Limited
120 Pentonville Road
London N1 9JN

British Library Cataloguing in Publication Data

A CIP record for this book is available from the British Library.

ISBN 0 7494 0501 5

Typeset by Laser Origination, Marine Court, St Leonards-on-Sea, Sussex.

Printed and bound in Great Britain by Martins of Berwick Ltd, Berwick upon Tweed.

Contents

This book is dedicated to Adrian Corfield, who cared so much about its aims and put them into practice with students right up until his untimely death.

Preface

This book has its origins in a project on student induction carried out by members of the Teaching and Learning Methods Group at Brighton Polytechnic's Business School. The group aimed to foster improvements in students' experience of their courses by encouraging innovation and improving the possibilities for learning.

Why was there a particular concern with student induction? Two main reasons. First, we identified the students' transitions into higher education as having critically important consequences for the quality of their entire experience of learning at this level. As one lecturer put it: 'Our students are at a *change fulcrum* when they arrive. It will not be easier to introduce new expectations at any other time.'

Second, the process of student induction is a potentially powerful vehicle for staff development in the student-centred approach to learning. We hoped that staff could gain experience of a wider repertoire of teaching and learning methods by their involvement in induction activities which they would subsequently 'import' into their subject teaching.

Eighteen months on, this has proved true in a substantial number of cases. We therefore decided to make the ideas and activities more widely available as a resource to others. We hope that it will encourage other institutions to give induction the priority that it deserves and to reap the benefits extending into the learning process as a whole. More particularly, we hope that this book will spur teachers, trainers and facilitators to ask themselves what students need from an induction programme, what they are currently getting, and what needs to be done differently.

Most of the activities can be carried out (or at least started) in lecture theatres or large classrooms, since that tends to be the main type of accommodation available in educational institutions.

We hope that you enjoy using and experimenting with the exercises in this book. And we hope you will find ways of taking what you learn from the experience into other aspects of work in facilitating student learning

Tom Bourner
Joyce Barlow

Acknowledgements

Members of the Teaching and Learning Methods Group were invited to contribute material for a student induction resource pack. The people in the group were Joyce Barlow, Jill Bourner, Tom Bourner, Mary Britton, Ian McGill, Marilyn Medforth, Geoff Pullen and Jenny Robertson.

Other people contributed to the activities either directly or indirectly: Hannah Hurst, Barry Lee-Scherer, Bill McQueen, Kevin Turner.

Contributions were received in a wide variety of forms. The form in which they have been included represents an attempt to meet the needs of the user whilst retaining the integrity of the original contributions. This has meant imposing a standard format on the activities whilst preserving the original terminology. So 'tutors' in some exercises become 'facilitators' in others. 'Students' sometimes become 'participants' or even 'group members'. Since this book is a resource to be dipped into and used rather than read as a continous text the resulting variety of style should not be a problem.

Many of the activities in this book are new. The majority have not previously appeared in print. For some of the activities it has been difficult or impossible to identify the original source. In those cases where the source is known we have done our best to give the appropriate credit. We would like to make special acknowledgement of the following sources:

John W. Newstrom and Edward E. Scannel (1980). *Games Trainers Play*, New York, McGraw-Hill.

Barrie Hopson and Mike Scally (1980). *Lifeskills Teaching Programmes*, Leeds, Lifeskills Associates.

Donna Brandes and Paul Ginnis (1986). *A Guide to Student-Centred Learning*, Oxford, Blackwell.

Graham Gibbs (1981). *Teaching Students to Learn*, Milton Keynes, Open University Press.

Trevor Habeshaw, Sue Habeshaw and Graham Gibbs (1987). *53 Interesting Ways of Helping Your Students to Study*, Bristol, Technical and Education Services Ltd.

If you find the activities in this handbook valuable then we suggest that you look at these books for additional ideas.

PART I

The Student Induction Approach

Introduction

First impresions count. When we meet someone for the first time we form impressions that affect our attitudes and our behaviour towards them. Sometimes we establish instant rapport; sometimes we decide early on to avoid them. First impressions are often confirmed by our subsequent experience. Sometimes though, despite unpromising first impressions, firm friendships are established.

On the basis of little experience we form expectations and make prophesies which become self-fulfilling. Those we warm to at the outset we offer friendship, and they confirm our initial impression by offering friendship in return (remember the kindegarten adage 'to make a friend, be a friend'. To those about whom we have reservations at the outset we present a defended or withdrawn face and then experience confirmation of our first impressions.

As it is with people so it is with organizations that we encounter for the first time. First impressions matter here too. Our attitudes and behaviour are much affected by our initial experience. Studies of labour turnover in organizations recognize what is termed an 'induction crisis' during which new entrants have a high propensity to quit. New employees who form a bad impression of their organization at the start and who are not in a position to quit are likely to form attitudes and adopt behaviours that benefit neither the organization nor themselves. The quality of their work and the quality of their employment experience is damaged.

For students joining an academic institution, first impressions are equally important. Their attitudes and behaviour are affected. These in turn affect the quality of their work and the quality of their learning experience. Our aim in compiling this book is to improve the quality of the learning experience of students.

This book focuses on the crucial stage of transition to a new institution and a more advanced stage of education. Many of the activities follow from our belief that in higher education students need to take more responsibility for their own learning: they need to know themselves as learners, to know what motivates them – and they need to develop skills to enable them to use the learning opportunities available. Higher education is less and less a matter of solitary application: it involves interacting and cooperating with fellow students in ways that are also relevant to life beyond the course.

The approach to induction in this guide is one of exercises and activities designed to develop skills. It starts with the need of students to feel part of the course and to develop friendships and good relationships with other students and staff. It offers ways of assisting the students to come to terms with the demands of their new course of study. It provides ways to help them to recognise that there are no universally correct ways of studying: the 'correct' way is what is right for them based on an awareness of how they personally learn best. From this base there are empowering exercises to help them begin to do this: confidence-building, listening skills, giving and receiving feedback, coope-rating and communicating.

Induction is a continuing process. Some of the exercises have a place at the beginning of the course. Some are applicable at stages within a course to improve skills and introduce new insights as a background to a new element of study. Others are appropriate for returning students, for example after a period of industrial placement, when students need to recognize and consolidate what they have learned and experienced and to integrate it with a further period of academic work.

This concept of induction may be unfamiliar in that it is not obviously linked to laying the foundations of subject knowledge. Rather it lays the foundations for being effective as a student and as a person. It is designed to help students get more value out of their experience of education, to improve their performance, and to provide a solid grounding for their future careers.

In the long term, these elements should be reflected in such performance indicators as:

- lower absenteeism from classes;
- lower student drop-out;
- better coursework results;
- better examination results.

In the short term, they should be reflected in more highly motivated, stimulated, energized, confident, curious, enthu-siastic students who are a pleasure to teach.

The Aims of an Induction Programme

At the broadest level, our aim in compiling this book is to improve the quality of students' overall experience at college or university, and in particular, their learning experience.

The titles of the book's different sections are an indication of the broad areas in which an introductory programme can help to lay the foundations of a good educational experience.

Introductions and getting acquainted

If students are to feel comfortable in a new situation they must be given an opportunity to establish their identity and feel personally secure. A crowd of people new to a college can be a 'lonely crowd' for a new student. Consequently, we have included material to help students to get to know each other, make new friends, develop a sense of group identity and gain some idea of each other's experience, interests, abilities and needs.

It is surprisingly common for this personal and social aspect to be discounted as having little bearing on the serious business of study. It is our experience that until this is sorted out it is much more difficult to get the student's attention for that 'serious business'.

Developing supportive relationships

This follows on from the idea of helping students gain some personal knowledge of each other. Our aim here is to establish a climate of mutual support and respect rather than criticism both among themselves and in their relationships with staff. Activities are included in this section which develop an appreciation of the benefits of cooperation and collaboration and an atmosphere in which students listen to each other and value each other's abilities as a resource. We encourage the formation of self-help groups and this means more dialogue, exploration of ideas and more stimulus from study than when students adopt a solitary, protective attitude to their work.

Acquiring relevant information

Obviously, information is crucial. The problem with some approaches to induction is that the student is bombarded with so much information – some of which is immediately relevant and some of which is not – that information overload occurs. Our approach is to help the students to identify both what they need to know and the sources of such information – and then to help them to acquire the information themselves.

From our experience the information needs seem to fall into the following main areas:

- *People:* the staff teaching on the course, fellow students (including students from other years), technicians, administrative staff, counsellors and so on.
- *The course:* its content, learning methods and assessment techniques and what demands it will make on students if they are to get the best from it.
- *The institution:* the immediate unit – the features of the department and how it fits into the pattern of the institution as a whole; the buildings and facilities where the student is based; other facilities which they are entitled to use such as libraries and recreational facilities.
- *The town:* in many cases students need to find their way around an unfamiliar place and find somewhere to live. They are often also interested in finding out what extra-curricular facilities are available for sport, culture, leisure and so on.

Coping with the problems of transition to higher education

The aim here is to prepare the student for dealing with the uncertainties and stresses associated with an unfamiliar form of learning. The activities in this section can help students form *realistic expectations* about the educational experience that they are about to encounter. This will enable them to identify the skills which they will need to develop and apply: study skills, quantitative expertise, computing and so on.

Students need to prepare themselves for prospective workloads in terms of course attendance, private study and written assignments. Less mature students, in particular, are likely to encounter difficulty coming to terms with the fact that they will have to motivate themselves and take responsibility for ensuring that they make progress. They also have to cope with a potentially wide range of learning methods including much more groupwork than at school and possibly such unfamiliar and challenging activities as role-play exercises and self or peer assessment.

Induction gives students the opportunity to bring their anxieties into full awareness, express them, and explore solutions with each other. This process can enable them to begin to feel at ease in the new environment much more quickly and then apply themselves wholeheartedly to the new phase of their life.

Developing learning skills

Learning skills are at the core of what students need in order to succeed in their higher-level studies. One of the first things to realize is that there is no magic formula – it is a case of helping the students to explore the options available and find what suits them. Induction can help in various ways:

- making students aware of the resources (human and material) available to them;
- arousing an interest in their own learning processes and an awareness of different learning styles;
- encouraging them to experiment with different methods of learning;
- developing skills in group work, project work, case studies;
- developing critical abilities in distinguishing quality written and oral work.

Empowering students

The exercises in this section address the need for personal skills and self-awareness in students. We see this as an end in itself and also as a means of underpinning their approach to their studies. This includes clarifying in their own minds what they want from their time at college: their priorities and their aspirations, during and beyond the course.

Some students bring a 'victim mentality' with them from schools where they were used to having things done for them and to them. We see induction programmes as having much potential in helping them to take charge of their own learning experience:

- *Assertiveness:* enabling students to be straightforward in their dealings with others, accepting personal responsibility for their experiences, ensuring that they get the benefits available from the course without resorting to aggression or infringing other people's rights.
- *Management skills:* helping students to appreciate the need for good time-management and self-organization in order to be effective and achieve their aims. This involves also helping students to become more aware of their own strengths and limitations.
- *Interpersonal skills:* helping students develop skills of interacting well with other people, including being able to be honest about their own feelings and able to express them appropriately, and learning to give and receive feedback constructively.

Making the most of the transition

It is a big decision to undertake a new and possibly very demanding course of study. Induction can play an important role in ensuring that the learning to be had from such a step is not lost.

Some Questions for Tutors and Course Teams

Here are some questions to help introduce the approach to induction adopted in this book. They are addressed to you as a member of staff teaching a course:

1 Who is responsible for ensuring that your students make the most of their transition into higher education? You? The students themselves? The institution? Anyone else?

2 What information do your students need to make a successful transition into higher education?

3 What procedures will you use to help your students to get to know each other in terms of their previous experience, abilities, interests and so on?

4 What can you do to establish a climate of mutual respect, support, informality and cooperation?

5 How will you engage your students in clarifying (and influencing) the objectives of the course?

6 How will you introduce yourself and describe your perception of your role, your special resources and limitations, your availability for consultation and so on?

7 How will you acquaint your students with the resources (material and human) available to them for accomplishing their learning objectives?

8 How can returning students be helped to get more out of their next year on the course than they did out of the previous year? And how can they be helped to learn from last year's experience to get more value out of the coming year?

9 Check your course objectives and then ask yourself which could be accomplished within an induction programme.

10 Which of the problems that were encountered last year on the course could be remedied within an induction programme?

How to Use the Activities

We recommend that you start by clarifying what it is you want to achieve in your induction programme. The next question is how best to do it. Consult the Index of Induction Activities at the back of the book to help you find an activity appropriate for what you want to accomplish.

There may be something there that fits the bill exactly and you can go ahead and use it straight away. You may not like an exercise as it stands but find that it gives you an idea for something else. Great! Adapt the original until you have got it so that it will work for you. Alternatively, using the original as a starting point, design a new activity to meet the particular needs of your group of students.

Having selected an exercise or modified one, it's yours to use as you see fit. There is no 'right' way to use the exercises. However, we would like to offer some suggestions.

Instructions

After providing the instructions for an exercise, encourage the participants to ask questions. It is helpful if the instructions are written large in summary form on flip chart paper (or on an OHP slide or on the blackboard) and displayed in a place where all the participants can see them.

Participation by staff

Participate in the exercises and discussion wherever possible. Staff 'model' the exercise for the participants by the nature of their own participation. The best time to give your own views is towards the end of the discussion after the students have had an opportunity to work through their own ideas and express them. Try to avoid giving the impression that after the students have expressed their views you are now giving them the 'correct' ideas – telling them what they should have said!

Discussion

Allow for a period of feedback and discussion after every exercise. Discussion is a very important part of experiencing an exercise. It allows the participants to articulate how they feel about what they have done, its lessons for them and anything that they intend to do as a consequence of participating. In fact, the leader may wish to facilitate the discussion through the following distinct and sequential stages:

1 Feelings about the exercise. The leader can initiate this stage in the discussion by simply asking "How do you feel about what we have just done?" This discussion can often stimulate insights within the participants and a greater level of self-awareness.
2 Thoughts about the exercise. The leader can ask something like "And what did you learn from this exercise".
3 Planning changes. The leader can ask questions along the lines of "So what things might you do differently as a result of what you have learned from this exercise?"

This sequence could also form the basis of a 'pyramiding' activity along the following lines:

1 In pairs, discuss (compare?) how you *felt* about doing the exercise.
2 Each pair join with another pair (to form a group of four) and discuss what you *learned* from the exercise.
3 Each group of four join with another group of four and discuss what things you might *do* differently as a result of doing the exercise.
4 Finally, a plenary discussion of what has emerged during this process.

The main role of the leader at this stage is to facilitate discussion between the participants. This can often best be accomplished by simply asking the sort of question that prompts further discussion (some of the exercises provide examples of the sort of questions that are likely to be productive).

It is usually pretty unproductive for the leader to be judgemental of the contributions to the discussion or to engage in dialogue with each of the participants. When students are speaking of how they feel, what they learned or what they are going to do, the leader does not know best – the student does. It is generally much better if the leader simply shows that each contribution to the discussion is valued.

Opting out

For whatever reason, a participant will sometimes not wish to engage in a particular activity. They may feel unwell or unconfident – or they may simply wish to reflect on what has come up from a previous activity. This should be respected as part of the process by which they are encouraged to take responsibility for their own learning.

One last thing

Try to make the induction activities fun for the students – and for yourself!

PART II

STUDENT INDUCTION ACTIVITIES

1 Introductions and Getting Acquainted

The first few weeks are particularly significant in an undergraduate's academic career. They constitute a period of very rapid adaptation and personal change, and a time for setting patterns that are likely to be of long standing: students can 'get off on the right foot' – or the wrong foot. (Parlett and Simons, 1976)

INTRODUCTIONS (1):
Interviews

Aims

- To begin to get to know one another.
- To develop confidence.
- To develop awareness of membership of a group.

Procedure

1 Group brainstorms things that they'd like to know about each other in the context of this group. Display the headings on a flip chart.
2 In pairs, one person interviews the other to gather this information (and anything else that the two think of and wish to share). Five minutes is probably about the right time for this part of the activity.
3 Interviewers remain where they are, while interviewees move round and interview someone that they have not previously met. Again, about five minutes.
4 Everyone prepares (organizes their notes, etc) to introduce the person they interviewed. About two minutes.
5 In turn, individuals address the group, introducing the person that they interviewed. About two minutes each.

Materials

- Flip chart and marker pen.
- Pen/pencil and paper for each participant.

INTRODUCTIONS (2):
Three Questions

Aim

To enable course members to become acquainted with each other.

Procedure

1 Ask course members to jot down three things that they would like to ask a person they are meeting for the first time. Suggest that they be creative and not ask the more obvious questions such as name and home town.

2 After allowing a few minutes, ask them to start moving around exchanging questions and answers. Encourage them to meet as many new people as possible.

3 Reassemble the entire group and have each person introduce themselves. As each individual is introduced, other course members are encouraged to add other pieces of information shared earlier. This will eventually provide a rich composite picture of each individual.

Possible discussion questions

- What were some of the more interesting things discovered about people? Would they have been discovered in 'normal' casual conversation? Why not?
- What were some of the more productive questions asked?
- What questions proved to be less productive? Why?

Source: Adapted from Newstrom and Scannell (1980).

INTRODUCTIONS (3):
What Sort of Person Am I?

Aim

To help course members get acquainted and feel more comfortable with each other.

Procedure

1 Outline to the course members the nature of this activity:

briefly explain what they will be asked to do in each of the steps.

2 Give each course member a safety pin (or a piece of masking tape plus a sheet of A4 paper with 'What sort of person am I?' written in large letters at the top. You may wish to point out the difference between the question 'What am I?' (a student, 19 years old, five foot, three inches tall, for example) and 'What sort of person am I?' (anxious, hopeless with machines, a creative person, etc). You may also wish to suggest that they avoid giving demographic data (age, gender, etc) in their answers.

3 Give ten minutes for each course member to write at least eight different answers to the question. (By asking for at least eight different answers course members will normally move beyond the superficial to more significant issues of self-disclosure.) Emphasize legibility, as course members need to be able to read their answers from a distance.

4 Ask course members to attach their completed sheet to the front of their clothing.

5 Course members circulate around the room as at a cocktail-party, but instead of speaking they read each other's answers to the question 'What sort of person am I?' Ask them to make eye-contact with each person they encounter.

6 At the end of this non-verbal stage, ask course members to return to a few different people they think it would be interesting to talk with.

Materials

Each course member requires a sheet of A4 paper with the question 'What sort of person am I?' written in large letters at the top, a pencil or pen and a safety pin (or a piece of masking tape).

Variations

- Include some *background music* during the non-verbal cocktail-party stage.
- Course members can speak during the cocktail-party stage. But you'll then need to place a time limit on each encounter (two minutes).
- There are various alternatives to the question 'What sort of person am I?' For example, 'Who am I?' Instead, course

members can be asked to complete an open-ended statement such as 'I'm the sort of person who . . .'.

- *Self-descriptive adjectives* (tired, creative, enthusiastic, confused) can be asked for instead of answers to a question. You could also have a second column of adjectives for answers to the question, 'How would I like to be?'
- At the end of the activity, course members can write their names on their sheets and *fix them to the wall* (you'll need plenty of bluetack if you decide to do this).
- This activity can be modified to become an exercise at the *end of a session*. In this case course members could be asked to write on their A4 sheets what they learned in the session or what they could do as a result of it.

INTRODUCTIONS (4):
'This is Who I Am' Sandwich Boards

Aim

To help course members get acquainted quickly in a way that raises energy levels.

Procedure

1 Give each course member a sheet of flip chart paper, and about two foot of string. Each of the sheets of paper has 'THIS IS WHO I AM' in large letters at the top. Place a box of marker pens (many different colours if possible) in the centre of the floor and allow ten minutes for course members to represent themselves using whatever *symbols* they choose.

2 Course members tie their completed sheets round their neck like sandwich boards.

3 They then circulate in cocktail-party fashion, but without speaking.

4 Ask the course members to make eye contact with each person that they encounter as well as looking at their sandwich board.

5 At the end of this non-verbal stage, ask course members to return to a few different people they think it would be interesting to talk with, based on their previous encounters.

Variations

Choose one of the following variations for all the course members or invite them to choose any variation they wish.

- Draw a pie chart with different-sized wedges to illustrate percentages of themselves devoted to certain life foci – for example, a time pie.
- Write a series of words on the sandwich board such as self-descriptive adjectives (enthusiastic, uninspired, tense, etc . . .).
- Draw pictures of animals, objects or music with which they identify.
- Look at the variations suggested for the previous activity, Introductions (3), for other variations that could also be used for this activity.

Materials

Flip chart sheets for each course member, a ball of string, scissors and marker pens.

GETTING ACQUAINTED:
Filling in the Gaps

Aim

To help individuals become better acquainted as members of a new group.

Procedure

1 Ask course members to form groups of three. Suggest strongly that they choose people that they do not yet know to form their group.
2 One group member spends three minutes telling the others about him/herself. The others then spend the next three minutes confirming what they thought they heard and 'filling in the gaps'. 'Filling in the gaps' involves drawing inferences and implications from what was said and left unsaid.
  The process is then repeated twice as each member of the group takes a turn in telling the others about him/herself.

Variations

- All three group members can take a turn in telling the others about themselves before the others have a chance to 'fill in the gaps'.
- Instead of providing an opportunity for each other to get acquainted, this process can be used to examine attitudes and perspectives on something that is relevant to course members. For example, 'What are my expectations, hopes and fears for the coming year?' or 'How I experienced my sandwich placement last year'.

LEARNING NAMES (1)

Aim

- To help learn each other's names.
- To break the ice and raise energy levels.
- To give a sense of achievement at an early stage.

Procedure

1 Ask how many members of the group have difficulty learning other people's names. Explain that the aim of this activity is to help them to learn each other's names.

2 Stand (or sit) with your students in a circle so that each member of the group can see the face of everyone else in the group.

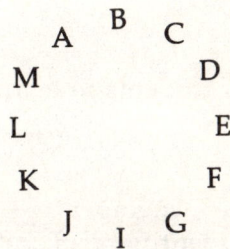

```
            B
        A       C
     M              D
     L              E
     K              F
        J       G
           I
```

3 Assuming that you are A, ask the name of the person, M, on your right. Then introduce him/her and yourself (loudly) to the person on your left, B, with the formula: 'Hello, my name's . . . and I'd like to introduce you to my friend . . .'

B turns to C and says: 'Hello, my name's B and I'd like to introduce you to my friends A and M'.

C turns to D and says: 'Hello, my name's C and I'd like to

introduce you to my friends B, A and M'.
And so on round the group.
(Remarkably, the only limit on the size of the group that this game can be used with seems to be determined by space rather than number of participants)

Possible discussion questions

- Why was it important to see each other's faces?
- How did you feel about being early/late in the round? And how do you feel about that now?
- How did you feel before it was your turn?
- How did you feel after you had done your bit?
- After it was your turn did you continue to be involved? Who gained most – those who went first or those who went last?
- How did you feel when someone couldn't remember your name?
- When someone couldn't remember your name did you want to help? Did you help? If so, how did you feel about that? If you were helped, how did you feel about that? From this can you distinguish between rescuing someone and enabling someone to learn?
- How did you feel about the member of staff when s/he proposed this activity?
- What did you learn from this exercise about how you learn?

LEARNING NAMES (2)

Aim

To help students to learn each other's names.

Procedure

Ask course members to select a personal characteristic that would help to identify them and to introduce it by rhyme or alliteration. Examples are:

- 'I'm Jovial Jill.'
- 'My name's Mike and I've got a bike.'
- 'I'm Sensible Syd.'
- 'I'm Tenacious Tom.'

Possible discussion questions

- How come it is easier to remember other people's names if you use this 'principle of association'.
- How can you use the principle of association to help you learn or remember other forms of knowledge on the course that you are just starting? (Possible answer: either by finding old concepts with which to associate new ideas or by reflecting on how the new knowledge relates to knowledge already held.)

Source: Newstrom and Scannell (1980).

GROUP MUGSHOTS

Aims

- To help the members of a group remember each other's names.
- To help develop group identity.

Procedure

Instead of conventional 'mug shot' pictures of individuals, produce group photographs of tutorial groups. A border round the photo allows participants names to be linked to their picture. Alternatively, let each participant write in his or her own forename in 'bubbles' with arrows.

FIRST-YEAR DIRECTORY

Aims

- To give new first-year students a record of some basic information about each other.
- To give them some help in making early contact with each other.

Procedure

1 Ask the students if they would like to compile a directory of some basic information about each other. If they say yes, suggest the following as a minimum:

- Surname
- Preferred first name
- Day and month of birthday
- Current address
- Current telephone number
- Home town
- Towns previously lived in
- Interests/activities/pastimes
- Some favourite things.

2 Encourage them to add to or delete from the above list.
3 Ask the students to write this information on a sheet (you may wish to prepare and distribute a form to get the information) and hand it in to you. Tell them that they can omit information in any of the categories if they so choose.

4 Collate the information and turn it into a directory so that everyone has a copy.

Variations

- Instead of providing the information manually, ask the students to key the information into a computer.
- Instead of collating the material yourself, use this activity as a group exercise. After discussing the desirability of the directory, tell them that if they can produce it in a form suitable for photocopying, you will get a copy made for every person in the class.

2 Developing Supportive Relationships

There are few obvious rules to follow – 'how to behave as a student' has to be picked up informally. Some fall into the new role easily, but for the majority there is a period of feeling unsettled, and personally insecure. (Parlett and Simons 1976)

MY SUPPORT NETWORK

Warning: Before undertaking this exercise it is advisable to ensure that work has already been done to develop supportive groups among the students.

Aim

To introduce students to the idea of a support network.

Procedure

1 Ask students to recall the last time they were studying. For most of them, this will probably be when they were at school.
2 Provide them with copies of the handout 'My support network'.
3 Allow enough time (about 20 minutes) for the students to complete the sections individually.
4 Ask students to discuss in small groups the results of doing this exercise. They can discuss the detail of what they have written or generalizations they can draw.
5 Plenary: Ask each group what generalizations emerged from their discussions.

Materials

Enough copies of the handout for all the students.

My Support Network: Handout

Recall the last time that you were engaged in a course of study. Write in the names of people who provided you with the different kinds of support at school/college and away from school/college. In the third column, make a note if you feel that you didn't get a certain type of support — and the reasons you didn't.

Types of support	At school/ college	Away from school/college	If I didn't get this support at all, why didn't I?
Someone I could always rely on			
Someone I just enjoyed chatting with			
Someone with whom I could discuss things we'd done on the course			
Someone who made me feel competent and valued			
Someone who gave me constructive feedback			
Someone who was a good source of information			
Someone I could depend on in a crisis			

Someone I could feel close to – a friend or intimate			
Someone I could share bad news with			
Someone I could share good news and good feelings with			
Someone who would introduce me to new ideas, new interests, new people			

What actions will I take?

At college:

Date(s) by:

Away from college:

Date(s) by:

ESTABLISHING COHESIVE GROUPS

Aim

To split a large group into small cohesive sub-groups.

Procedure

1 Ask course members to number themselves off, 'one, two, one, two' etc to make two large groups.
2 Ask all the 'ones' to move to the right side of the room and the 'twos' to go to the left.
3 Ask each of the two large groups to look at the members of the other group and mentally rank them by how well they know them. Each of the 'ones' then invites someone from the other group that they do not know to form a pairing. As each pair forms they move to another part of the room.
4 Split the pairs into two groups: half on one side of the room and half on the other.
5 The pairs discuss for up to three minutes which pair on the other side of the room they would like to join. Then ask one pair to invite a pair from the other side of the room to join them in making a foursome. Introduce the 'rule' that, at this stage, pairs may decline invitations to form a foursome. Repeat with successive pairs until the process is complete.
6 After discussion of not more than three minutes, a foursome from one side of the room asks a foursome from the other side of the room to join them in forming an eightsome. In this phase too an invitation to join may be declined. When all the foursomes have been chosen then the process is complete.
7 The eightsomes formed in the above way can now participate in various groupwork activities (eg as syndicate groups). However, it makes sense to spend some time processing the experience of selecting and being selected, the effect of the process on the composition of the groups, the effect of group composition on performance of groups, etc.

Variations

- At each stage in the process of group formation, questions can be provided to focus on the experience of group formation. For example: 'We chose you because . . . ' 'When you chose us, I felt . . . ' 'At the moment I'm feeling . . . '.

- After discussing the effects of the process on group composition and the effect of group composition on group performance invite individuals to swap with persons from other groups to achieve a balanced representation of such factors as gender, age, nationality, etc. You may want to brainstorm possible factors that could be relevant.

GROUP MOVEMENT

Aims

- To create some physical movement among the students.
- To add opportunities for additional dimensions of student interaction.

Procedure

Many students in a new environment will find a favourite seat or area and cling to it for the duration of the first week (or even the whole of a four-year course). The following two methods can be used to encourage movement among the students.

1 Ask course members to select the person whom they:

- know least about,
- identify most closely with, or
- feel most in disagreement with,

and seek out that person as their conversational partner for the next few minutes.
2 Sort course members into different physical locations according to their different views on a topic. As reports are presented from the subgroups, allow converts to join other groups.

Source: Adapted from Newstrom and Scannell (1980).

INTERVIEW WITH YOU

Aims

- To give each student an opportunity to learn more about how

one of his or her classmates thinks and feels.
- To draw pairs of students closer together.

Procedure

1 Introduce the activity in this way:
'Today we are going to get to know someone in the class a lot better than we do now. We will do this through questions. Each of you will have a partner to interview. I will give you a set of questions to ask each other.
'Each person in the pair will have a number, either one or two. For the first round number 1 will ask the questions and number 2 will answer. Then number 2 will ask the same questions and number 1 will answer. For subsequent questions, reverse who answers the question first and second.
'Now pair off with someone you have not had much opportunity to get to know very well. I will then pass out the questions and you can begin.'

2 The initial questions on the sheet should be of a less personal nature, gradually building up to the more personal ones later. When the interviews are completed, the students are to tell each other in what ways they feel they know each other better. As a total class, the students can discuss their reactions to this activity. They can also talk more generally about how to get to know people better.

3 Create questions that are appropriate for the levels of your classes. There are some suggestions below in the form of incomplete statements ('sentence stems' or 'sentence stubs'). Either compose questions based on these sentence stubs or just have each person complete the statement as it is given.

4 You can ask students to suggest other statements to complete. Be certain to maintain a positive focus in all of them, and include statements which involve talking about one's partner.

Materials

A set of sentence stubs such as the following:

- I am a person who ....
- I am happiest when ....
- I would like to be ....
- One thing that I can do well is ....

- A friend can count on me to...
- I like people who ....
- I'm proud of myself when ....
- In ten years I ....
- One thing that I like about myself is...
- I like to daydream about..
- The person I most admire is ....
- My favourite pastime is...
- It's really fun to..
- If I were given a lot of money to spend, I'd ....
- Right now I feel ....
- One of my strongest points is..
- I can see that one of your strong points is...
- One way that I could enjoy spending time with you is ....
- What I like best about you is ....
- If I could have one wish come true, I'd ask for...........................

BIRTH ORDER

Aims

To gain perceptions about oneself and one's classmates along a new dimension.

To discover commonalities and new understandings among groups of students in the class to draw them closer together.

Procedure

1 Ask students to answer these questions for you on a sheet of paper to be handed in.
   - How many brothers do you have?
   - How many sisters do you have?
   - Are you the youngest or the oldest child in the family?
   - If you are a middle child, make a list showing all of your brothers and sisters and where you fit in according to your age. For example as follows:

Brother (oldest)
Brother
ME
Sister
Brother (youngest)

- State here if you are an only child.

2 When you have this information from everyone, divide the students into groups according to their birth order or other commonalities. These are examples of such groups:
   - Oldest child
   - Youngest child
   - Only child
   - Middle child in small family
   - Middle child in large family.

3 Notice whether there are other commonalities such as the youngest child (female) with all male siblings. Try to keep the groups from becoming excessively large by finding a subdivision of the commonalities of the larger groups. In a class where nine students are the oldest child a way to subdivide them could be a division between the oldest of three or more children and the oldest of two children.

4 Combine students who do not fit into a group with the one closest to their situation.

5 The exercise begins by placing students in their birth order groups and explaining how each group was determined. Tell the class:

'Many things influence our personality, feelings and attitudes. One of these is our place in the order in which children were born in our family.

'You are now in a group according to your birth order in your family. Try to find out what things you have in common with the others in your group. Talk about such things as your feelings, experiences, attitudes, values, personality, how you handle certain situations and how these may be due to your common birth order.

'See what similarities you can find in these areas in your group. For example, you can look at your feelings about independence, competition, responsibility, desire for attention etc, and how these relate to your birth position. In other words, what did your birth order mean to you and what positive effects did it have on you?

'Write down the similarities your group discovers. Later you will report your findings to the total class. You can share some things about yourself and ask others in your group whether they feel or behave similarly. In this way you will identify what things your group has in common'.

6 Allow about ten to 15 minutes for the class to work on this in groups while you circulate to each group. Then ask all the groups to report their findings to see what similarities or differences there are. As the reports are given, ask questions of the class to determine whether they are hearing the key points.

POSITIVE FEEDBACK

Aim

To encourage the giving of positive feedback.

Procedure

1 Divide the group into pairs.
2 Ask each person to write four or five positive things that they have noticed about their partner (this might include, for example, neat dresser, pleasant voice, good listener, etc).
3 After a few minutes of writing, an open discussion follows for each group of two, wherein the observer states what he or she wrote about the other.

Possible discussion questions

- Were you comfortable with this exercise? If not, why?
- What would make it easier to *give* positive feedback to others? (Develop a close relationship first; provide validating evidence; choose an appropriate time).
- What would make it easier for us to *receive* positive feedback from others? (Practise accepting it with grace; decide to really consider its validity before challenging it; allow yourself to feel good about it.)

Source: Newstrom and Scannell (1980).

TIME TO SHARE

This activity is best used where participants have had the opportunity to interact with each other for a reasonable time.

Aims

- To give individuals permission to give positive feedback.
- To encourage individuals to share positive qualities with others.

Procedure

1 Divide the group into pairs then introduce the session by saying that we all need recognition and 'positve strokes'.
2 Ask each person to tell his or her partner the following:

- One physical feature that is particularly nice about his or her partner.
- One or two personality traits that are unusually pleasant about his or her partner.
- One or two talents or skills that are noteworthy about his or her partner.

3 Suggest that each person record their partner's feel-ings, thoughts and feedback and save them to read when they are having a bad day.

Possible discussion questions

- Why is it difficult for many of us to give each other a compliment?
- Why is it that most people are quick to give a negative comment but find it hard to say positive things to each other?

Source: Newstrom and Scannell (1980).

COOPERATIVE GAME

Aims

- To develop cooperation and trust.
- To have some fun.

Procedure

1 The students (at least 12) are asked to discover (in pairs?) a way in which everyone in the room could simultaneously sit on each other's knees.
2 One (possibly the only) solution is for everyone to stand in a circle and then simultaneously lower themselves onto the knees of the person behind.
3 When someone suggests this solution (if necessary with heavy prompting from the tutor) encourage some discussion of its feasibility then suggest that the group test it empirically as follows:

First, the group stands in a very tight circle and each person puts their hands on the shoulders of the person in front.
Second, at an agreed signal, everyone lowers him/herself onto the knees of the person behind and then at another agreed signal they stand up. (It is worth doing this several times.)

NB Collapses are likely.

Possible discussion questions

In what conditions is this solution viable? (Smallest number of participants, attitude of participants etc.)

Variations

- Everyone stretches their arms together.
- Everyone leans slightly towards the centre of the circle and raises the leg on the outer side of the circle (a 'Flying Arkright').
- Stepping alternately with right and left feet (not easy).

3   Acquiring Relevant Information

Preparing students for transitions will obviously involve getting them to think forward into what they expect of the new situation and what might be expected of them by others.

The more information students have on the above the less stressful the transition is likely to be, though all transitions naturally involve some stress.

Getting the students to collect as much data about what others expect, what society expects, the norms, 'language' and behaviours that are appropriate in the new situation gives them a chance to ask:

'Will I need to change in any way?'
'Do I want to change in any way?'
'Am I prepared to change in any way?'
Hopson and Scally (1980).

INFORMATION NEEDS

Aim

To identify information that the students want about the course, department or institution.

Procedure

This group discussion method is called the 'nominal group technique'. It encourages participation by the shyer or more passive members of a group and results in a set of prioritized recommendations. It has been recommended as a method for conducting course evaluation exercises.

1 Ask the students to spend a few minutes individually writing down about four or five brief responses to the question: 'What are the most important things that you want to know about the course, department or institution?'

2 Divide the students into groups of about 12. Give each group flipchart paper, bluetack and a marker pen. Ask each group to form a single composite list of the items while they are recorded on the flipchart. This can easily be done by sharing the items in a 'round robin' fashion (one response per person each time).

Criticism of the comments of others is discouraged but *clarification* in response to questions is encouraged.

3 Each person then evaluates the items on the group list and individually 'votes' for them, giving 5 for the most important, 4 for the next most important and so on.

4 'Votes' for each item are then collected within the group and tabulated. A group report is prepared showing the comments receiving the highest scores.

5 The flipchart sheets of each group are then fixed to the wall as an 'agenda' for information to be sought throughout the induction programme.

Possible discussion questions

- For what types of problem is this method of groupwork likely to be particularly useful?
- What are its limitations?

Variations

- Use the results of this exercise to brief the head of department or course leader for when they talk to the students.
- The nominal group technique is a potentially valuable teaching method. It can be adapted to all sorts of questions such as 'What are the main differences between school and your present course?' or 'What are some of the important things that should be in a good essay/report/presentation?'

Materials

Flipchart paper, blutack and marker pens for each group.

Source: Kevin Turner (Department of Business Management, Brighton Polytechnic).

SWAP SHOP

Aims

- To obtain new ideas and information.
- To encourage group participation.

Procedure

1 Everyone in the class is asked to bring to the next session at least one piece of information about the course (or the department or the institution or town) that would be useful to a new student. (They could alternatively be asked to bring to

the next session a suggestion for a piece of informa
new student would find useful).

2 As each person contributes his or her piece of information to the group, a panel of 'experts' (three selected class members) instantly rate the ideas by holding up the appropriate index cards (1 to 10, with 10 being the highest). The facilitator tabulates the total and announces the winners at the end of the time period (and possibly awards a small prize such as a bottle of wine).

Possible discussion questions

- How many people gained at least one useful piece of information?
- Did the process spark off in your mind any ideas for additional information that you want?
- What do you like and what do you dislike about this as a method of generating information and doing groupwork?

Materials

Three sets of ten index cards, each set numbered 1 to 10.

Source: Adapted from Newstrom and Scannell (1980).

TREASURE HUNT

Aims

- To discover information about the course, department, institution or town that will be useful in the student's education.
- To engage course members in a task-orientated activity so they can begin developing a team identity and cohesiveness.

Procedure

1 Divide the course members into teams of about six.
2 Provide or develop a minimal set of ground rules (eg the time limit for completing the treasure hunt; they must not sabotage other groups) and a list of objects or information to obtain. It is best to include items that are feasible to obtain, but which are likely to require ingenuity or collaborative effort within the group to be successful (see below). Including some items that can be found in the course handbook provides an incentive to read it.

3 Score the groups on the basis of the number of items obtained and announce the winning group. Consider awarding a prize.

Possible discussion questions

- How did the group organize itself to conduct the task? (Were individuals or pairs assigned to specific items, or was everyone trying to do everything?) How was this method chosen? How successful was it?
- What will you do differently when you are assigned a more serious learning task as a group?

Materials

List of 'treasure' items. (NB the number of copies – one or many – of the list provided to each group might also serve as a factor that contributes to the various group approaches.)

Possible items for treasure hunt

- The opening hours of the library
- The name of the building in which the Careers Advisory Service is located
- The number of cinemas in town
- The telephone extension of the departmental office
- The names of three student counsellors
- The name of the licensee of the closest public house
- How many members of staff in the department have a surname beginning with the letter 'B'.

(A list of items for the treasure hunt could be constructed from the information that the students say they want – using the nominal group exercise).

STUDENT INTERVIEWS

Aims

- To familiarize students with staff and their expectations and attitudes about the course.
- To find out information about the course.

Procedure

1 Brainstorm things that students would like to find out about

was the method chosen? How successful was it?
- What would you do differently if you were starting again?
- How does your leaflet differ from those produced by the other groups? What information is contained within your leaflet that is not contained in any of the other leaflets?

Variations

- After each group has received copies of the other groups' leaflets, have a second round of this exercise. In this second round, each group can utilize the ideas of the other groups. Discussion after this second round can focus on the diffe-rences in the group process and differences in the final outputs and reasons for the differences.

Materials

Course handbooks or course submission documents.

QUIZ

Aim

To familiarize the students with information about the course, department, institution or town.

Procedure

1 Divide the students into two teams. The teams elect a panel of four and devise fiendish (but fair) questions about the course, the department, the institution or town.
2 Nominate two judges to:

- vet the questions and throw out unfair ones
- chair the quiz and select questions to ask
- judge whether the questions have been answered fairly
- keep the score

3 Tape-record a fragment of the radio programme *Brain of Britain* for students to illustrate the style of the questions that may be asked (optional).
4 The questions of one team are addressed to the other team. (Ask team members to contribute to a prize?)

Materials

> Recording of a fragment of the radio programme *Brain of Britain* (optional).

Source: Gibbs and Jaques (1987).

THE STUDENT AS EXPERT

Aims

- To familiarize the students with information about the course, department, institution or town.
- To help students to become aware of each other as learning resources.
- To raise self-confidence and self-esteem of students by enabling each to acquire special expertise in an area.

Procedure

1 After the information needs of the students have been identified (by brainstorming, nominal group technique or whatever) ask each student to take responsibility for becoming an expert in an area that covers one particular information need. For example, if an identified information need is to know whether coursework contributes to course assessment then someone could become the class expert on student assessment.

2 Put a list of student names with their associated expertise on the course notice board so that everyone in the class is aware of who the class expert is on a particular topic.

3 Towards the end of the induction programme, ask each student to speak for three minutes on his or her specialist area, giving a few important bits of information and some useful sources of information on the topic.

A few other approaches

It is clear from student feedback that too many people do too much talking at the students in their first week of college. This is understandable: there is much information that staff wish them to have. It is easy, however, for 'information overload' to occur, when all the information is received through the same one channel or medium. This section has identified some alternative

ways to convey the information. Here are a few more suggestions:

- Ask the students to produce an organization chart of the
  institution or the department.
- Ask the students to compile a fact sheet of useful information that will be distributed to new students as part of next
  year's induction programme.
- Ask second – and/or subsequent – year students to give new
  students a guided tour (individually or in groups).
- Ask the students to complete a glossary of initials that they
  encounter during their first week at the institution.
- Spot the error. Ask students to choose sections in student
  guides. Photocopy these for the class and see how many
  errors the students can find in them.
- Ask the students to compile a list of possible resources for
  finding out information about the course, the department or
  the institution.

4   Coping with the Problems of Transition into Higher Education

Here is Edward Bear, coming downstairs now, bump, bump, bump, bump, on the back of the head, behind Christopher Robin. It is, as far as he knows, the only way of coming downstairs, but sometimes he feels that there really is another way, if only he could stop bumping for a moment and think of it. (A. A. Milne, *Winnie the Pooh*)

PRECONCEIVED IDEAS AND FEARS

Aims

- To reduce misconceptions about the course.
- To facilitate disclosure of fears.

Procedure

Form course members into small groups of about four to six persons. Provide each group with a flipchart and pen and ask each group to select a recorder. Ask them to quickly respond to the question 'What fears, concerns or preconceived notions did you have prior to coming here today?' After a brief period to gather responses, ask the reporters to present their lists to the entire group. This gives a good opportunity for the member of staff running the session to empathize with the needs of the course participants as well as providing support and reassurance by using items to indicate how the course does or does not relate to the concerns.

Possible discussion questions

- What can staff do to diminish those concerns?
- What can students do to deal with some of the issues raised?
- Who else can help?

Materials

Flipcharts and pens.

Source: Adapted from Newstrom and Scannel (1980).

TRANSITIONS

Aims

- To show that all transitions have elements in common.
- To help students identify their personal style of coping with transitions.
- To provide the opportunity to acquire additional strategies for coping with their current transition into higher education and also future transitions.

Procedure

1 Introduce the class to the idea that starting their course is a 'transition' in their lives (a transition into higher education).
2 Ask the class to identify (brainstorm?) previous life transitions that they have passed through in their lives so far. These could include learning to walk, starting primary school, starting secondary school, moving house, changing schools, losing a good friend who moved away, having a new baby in the family and so on.
3 Ask members of class first to note which of the list applies to them and, second, to select one transition that they feel that they can learn most from. Then ask each person to 'interview' another person using the format:

- What do you remember of the transition?
- How were you different from before?
- Did it cause you any difficulties?
- Did anything or anybody help? If so how?
- When did you feel comfortable again and accept the new situation?

4 After this, the roles are reversed – the interviewee becomes the interviewer and vice versa.
5 Plenary – to provide an opportunity for sharing after this stage of the exercise.

6 Ask the class to do another round in which they contemplate their current transition into higher/further education:

- What are you moving from?
- What are you moving to?
- How will you behave differently?
- What difficulties might there be?
- How can you help yourself or get help?
- What will you miss or lose?
- What do you stand to gain?

7 Plenary – to provide an opportunity for sharing after this stage of the exercise.
8 Introduce the notion of a 'transition style' as the personal way that an individual has of coping with transitions.
9 Ask individuals in small groups (foursomes?) to use the range of their own past experience to identify their own 'transitional styles'. It may be helpful in doing this to ask themselves the following questions:

- How typically do I prepare for transitions if I can forsee them?
- How do I tend to react during transitions?
- What feelings do I tend to get?
- How do I cope with these?
- Do I use others as resources?
- Do I treat the transition as a phase that will pass?
- Am I able to see opportunities to be gained as a result of the transition?
- Can I identify what I learn from the experience and how I am different?
- Do I manage to limit the number of transitions that I have to cope with at any one time?

10 Split back into pairs to focus on answering the question 'Am I happy with my transition style or do I want to change any element of it?' and the development of 'action plans' to produce the required change.

Source: Hopson and Scally (1980).

TRANSITION COPING SKILLS
QUESTIONNAIRE

Aims

- To help students to identify their personal styles of coping with transitions.
- To produce awareness of elements that can help in coping with transitions.
- To provide an opportunity to acquire additional strategies for coping with future life transitions.
- To given an opportunity to identify what useful self-awareness can come from a transition experience.

Procedure

1 Introduce the idea of life transitions in general and transition into higher education in particular.
2 Facilitate a class discussion on the nature of transitions. You may want to introduce some of the following themes:

- Are there common elements that are shared by all transitions?
- Are there common ways that we all feel when passing through a transition?
- To what extent do transitions offer the opportunity for personal growth and development?
- Do we all tend to respond to transitions in the same way?

3 Distribute the 'transition coping skills questionnaire' (see below) to all the students.

Materials

Enough copies of the 'transition coping skills questionnaire' for all the students.

Source: Hopson and Scally (1980).

Transition Coping Skills: Questionnaire

Section 1: Knowing myself

Questions	Answers or comments
A Is this transition something that I wanted to happen?	
B Am I somebody who makes things happen rather than sits back and lets things happen?	
C Do I know what I'd like to get out of this new situation?	
D Do I know what I do not want from this new situation?	
E If I feel under stress in this new situation do I know what I can do to help myself?	

Section 2: Knowing my new situation

A Do I know how I will be expected to behave in the new situation?	
B Do I know how I can get information about my new situation?	

Section 3: Knowing others who can help

DO I KNOW OTHER PEOPLE A – on whom I can depend in a crisis?	
B – with whom I can discuss concerns?	
C – to whom I feel close (a friend)?	
D – who can recognize my strengths and help me to feel valued?	
E – who can give me the information that I need?	
F – who will challenge me and make me face the things that I need to face?	
G – with whom I can share good times and good experiences?	

Section 4: Looking after myself

A Do I have places, people or situations which give me a secure base?	
B Do I give myself a treat if I am going through a bad patch	

C Do I have people who will 'take care' of me at times when I need them?	
D Am I able to 'survive' (ie keep myself going when times are hard) until the better times come?	

Section 5: Leaving the past behind

A Do I hang on to what is past or easily leave one situation and move to another?	
B Do I often think 'It's not fair. This shouldn't happen to me'?	
C Am I able to express anger or other strong feelings in ways that help?	

Section 6: Looking for benefits (gains)

A Am I able to find at least one good thing that I have gained by moving into my new situation?	
B Am I able to list various oppor-- tunities I now have, which I didn't have or hadn't thought of before?	

C Have I learned something new about myself? If so, what?	
D Am I able to describe the ways that I am different from how I was before?	
E What have I learned that will be useful in the future?	

REDUCING THE STRESS OF TRANSITION INTO HIGHER EDUCATION

Aims

- To use the group resources to reduce the stress associated with the transition into higher education.
- To develop cooperation and open exchange in coping with the stress of entering higher education.

Procedure

1 Distribute copies of the following handout (Holmes and Rahe's 'social readjustment rating scale') and ask the students to identify all the stressors that are likely to affect new entrants into higher education. (Check that there are no additional ones that students regard as important not mentioned on the Holmes and Rahe scale.)

2 Each member lists their five most important stressors (including any not mentioned on the Holmes and Rahe scale) in order of importance.

3 Groups of about five are formed and group members are asked to explain their two most important stressors to the rest of the group. The frequency of each stressor selected within the group is noted.

4 The groups meet and the results for each group are displayed. Encourage illustrations and examples.

5 A frequency distribution of stressors across all the groups is then constructed from the results from the groups.

6 Take the most frequently occurring stressor. Brainstorm possible first steps for reducing it.

Variation

Individuals choose which stressor to work with and group accordingly.

Trios are formed within the groups and work briefly to devise practical plans for implementing first steps for reducing the stressor.

In sixes, examine each other's plans.

Each trio reports its refined strategy before task groups form to make concrete the first steps. Who will do what, where, by when? 'When shall we meet again to evaluate and revise if necessary?'

Reducing the Stress of Transition into Higher Education: Handout

Holmes and Rahe ('The social readjustment rating scale' in *Journal of Psychosomatic Research* 11, 213–18, 1967) developed a 'social readjustment rating scale' which gives some indication of the amount of stress an individual has incurred over the last 12 to 18 months. According to their research, the life changes represented below, along with their weighted scores, were remarkably consistent across different cultures: Japan, Hawaii, Central America, Peru, Spain, France, Belgium, Switzerland and Scandinavia. The correlation between items ranged from 0.65 to 0.98 across all the cultures.

A notable feature of the transition into higher education is not that it is associated with the very high stressor life events but that it is associated with a fair number of 'middle range' stressors.

	Life event	Stress Rating
1	Death of a spouse	100
2	Divorce	73
3	Marital separation from mate	65
4	Detention in jail or other institution	63
5	Death of a close family member	63
6	Major personal injury or illness	53
7	Marriage	50
8	Being fired at work	47
9	Marital reconciliation with mate	45
10	Retirement from work	45
11	Major change in the health of a family member	44
12	Pregnancy	40
13	Sexual difficulties	39
14	Gaining a new family member (eg through birth or adoption)	39
15	Major business readjustment (eg bankruptcy, merger etc)	39
16	Major change in financial state (much worse off or much better off than usual)	38
17	Death of a close friend	37

18	Changing to a different line of work (or different area of study)	36
19	Major changes in the number of arguments with spouse	35
20	Taking on a mortgage greater than $10,000 (eg purchasing a home, business etc)	31
21	Foreclosure on a mortgage or loan	30
22	Major change in responsibilities at work (eg promotion, demotion, lateral transfer)	29
23	Son or daughter leaving home (eg marriage, attending college etc)	29
24	In-law troubles	29
25	Outstanding personal achievement	28
26	Wife beginning or ceasing work outside the home	26
27	Beginning or ceasing formal schooling	26
28	Major change in living conditions	25
29	Revision of personal habits (dress, manners, associations, etc)	24
30	Trouble with the boss	23
31	Major change in working hours or conditions	20
32	Change in residence	20
33	Changing to a new school	20
34	Major change in usual type and/or amount of recreation	19
35	Major change in church activities (eg a lot more or a lot less than usual	19
36	Major change in social activities	18
37	Taking on a loan of less than $10,000 (eg purchase of car, TV or freezer etc)	17
38	Major change in sleeping habits (a lot more or a lot less sleep, or a change in the part of day when asleep)	16
39	Major change in the number of family get-togethers (a lot more or a lot fewer than usual)	15
40	Major change in eating habits (a lot more or a lot less food intake, or very different meal hours or surroundings)	15
41	Vacation	13
42	Christmas	12
43	Minor violations against the law (eg traffic ticket, disturbing the peace etc)	11

DEVELOPING SKILLS FOR COPING WITH TRANSITIONS

Aim

To identify skills that would be useful in coping with the first year of higher education.

Procedure

1 Distribute copies of the skills list and ask the students to complete it.
2 Ask the students to consider those skills which they have ranked 1 or 2 (never or seldom good at). Ask them to consider, 'How might development of this skill help you to become more effective in your first year of higher education?'
3 Ask them to identify the one or two potentially most important skill(s) that are currently underdeveloped.
4 Ask them to form pairs and devise a programme to develop this skill. It might be helpful to list when, where and with whom or how often they will do something, exactly what it is that they will do and to arrange to meet their partner to report back and discuss how the programme is progressing.

Materials

Enough copies of the handout for all the students.

Source: Adapted from University of Nottingham M Ed (Human Relations) course.

Developing Skills for Coping with Transition: Skills List Handout

Go through each of the skills listed and rate yourself:
How good am I at using this skill?

1	2	3	4	5
Never good at it	Seldom	Some-times	Often	Always good at it

1 2 3 4 5   (1)   *Starting a conversation:* Talking to someone about light topics and then leading into more serious topics

1 2 3 4 5   (2)   *Carrying on a conversation:* Opening the main topic, elaborating it and responding to the reactions of the person you are talking to.

1 2 3 4 5   (3)   *Ending a conversation:* Letting the other person know that you have been paying attention, and then skilfully closing the conversation appropriately.

1 2 3 4 5   (4)   *Listening:* Paying attention to people, trying to understand them, and letting them know that you are trying.

1 2 3 4 5   (5)   *Expressing encouragement:* Telling someone when you believe that they can try something that they are not sure they can do.

1	2	3	4	5	(6)	*Expressing appreciation:* Letting another person know that you are grateful for something they have done for you.
1	2	3	5	5	(7)	*Giving positive feedback:* Telling someone that you like something about their actions.
1	2	3	4	5	(8)	*Giving negative feedback:* Telling someone that you don't like something about their actions.
1	2	3	4	5	(9)	*Asking for help:* Requesting assistance from someone that you believe is able to help you in a difficult situation that you have not been able to manage by yourself.
1	2	3	4	5	(10)	*Giving instructions:* Clearly explaining to someone how you would like a specific task done.
1	2	3	4	5	(11)	*Expressing a complaint:* Telling someone that they are responsible for creating a particular problem for you and attempting to find a solution to the problem.
1	2	3	4	5	(12)	*Persuading others:* Attempting to convince others that your ideas are better than theirs.
1	2	3	4	5	(13)	*Following instructions:* Carrying out directions in a competent manner and giving your reactions.

1 2 3 4 5	(14)	*Responding to persuasion:* Carefully considering another person's ideas, weighing them against your own and then deciding which course of action will be best for you in the long run.
1 2 3 4 5	(15)	*Responding to failure:* Working out what went wrong and what you can do about it so that you can be more successful in the future.
1 2 3 4 5	(16)	*Responding to contradictory messages:* Recognizing and dealing with the confusion that results when a person tells you one thing but says or does another.
1 2 3 4 5	(17)	*Responding to a complaint:* Dealing fairly with another person's dissatisfaction with a situation attributed to you.
1 2 3 4 5	(18)	*Setting a goal:* Deciding on what you want to accomplish and judging whether your plan is realistic.
1 2 3 4 5	(19)	*Gathering information:* Deciding what specific information you need and asking the appropriate people for the information.
1 2 3 4 5	(20)	*Concentrating on a task:* Making those preparations that will enable you to get a job done efficiently.
1 2 3 4 5	(21)	*Evaluating your abilities:* Examining your accomplishments fairly and honestly in order to decide how competent you are in a particular skill.

1 2 3 4 5	(22)	*Preparing for a stressful conversation:* Planning ahead to present your point of view in a conversation which may be difficult.
1 2 3 4 5	(23)	*Setting problem priorities:* Deciding which of several priorities is most urgent and should be worked on first.
1 2 3 4 5	(24)	*Making requests:* Asking the appropriate person for what you need or want.
1 2 3 4 5	(25)	*Relaxation:* Learning to calm down and relax when you are tense.
1 2 3 4 5	(26)	*Responding to praise:* Letting a person know that you are pleased with their praise and that you appreciate it.
1 2 3 4 5	(27)	*Managing time:* Setting priorities, planning and meeting deadlines. Not getting into situations where you regret 'wasted' or badly used time.
1 2 3 4 5	(28)	*Negotiation:* Arriving at an agreement which is satisfactory to you and to another person who has taken a different position.
1 2 3 4 5	(29)	*Assertiveness:* Standing up for yourself by letting others know what you want, how you feel, or what you are thinking about something.

ROLES OF A TUTOR

Aim

To develop an understanding (contract) between the tutor and students about the role of the tutor in higher education and how it might differ from previous student experience of teachers at school.

Procedure

1 Invite the students to express the various roles, attitudes and behaviours they expect (or wish) the tutors to exhibit for them. List these on a flipchart or chalkboard.
2 Then share a previously prepared set of your intended roles. A sample set (for illustration) is shown in the handout. Then proceed to reconcile the two lists.

Possible discussion questions

- What do you expect in a tutor that I do not intend to provide? What is the source of your expectations? (Prior educational experience? Wishful thinking?)
- What do I intend to provide that you did not expect?
- Do you anticipate any problems reconciling your expectations with my objections? If so, what can I or you do to prevent such problems?

Variations

This format can be used for addressing students' expectations about other aspects of higher education. For example: What is the difference between being a pupil at school and being a student in higher education? How do teaching/learning methods differ between school and higher education? Apart from passing the course, what do you hope to get out of your experience of higher education? What attitudes are likely to enable you to get most out of your experience of higher education?

Materials

Handout or transparency with list of intended roles.

Source: Adapted from Newstrom and Scannell (1980).

Roles of a Tutor in Higher Education: Illustrative Handout

1 Challenges thinking

2 Summarizes

3 Shares ideas

4 Provides handouts

5 Serves as a model

6 Raises questions

7 Guides discussion

8 Restates ideas

9 Provides constructive criticism

REACHING CONCLUSIONS WITH THE DELPHI METHOD

Aims

- To illustrate how others can be a helpful resource in coping with problems and reaching better decisions.
- To introduce the Delphi Method as a structured approach to convergence of informed opinions.

Procedure

The Delphi Method is an approach to estimation and prediction that involves the selection of a range of informed experts, each of whom has a genuine interest in the issue in question as follows:

- Each expert is asked for his or her best guess *independently*.
- Feedback (group average and frequency distribution) is provided and the process is repeated several times.
- A convergence of thought usually emerges which is usually more accurate than most of the individual estimates.

1 Ask the group to estimate the proportion of students who failed to complete the first year successfully last year (or the proportion of students who got first-class degrees or the proportion of students who found employment in the accounting sector of the economy). The Students in Higher Education Database (SHED) in the Centre for Business Research at Brighton Polytechnic is a useful source of information on topics that are likely to be of interest to the students.

2 Explain the Delphi method (as above) and then ask each group to apply it to the estimation asked for in 1. Ask them to iterate the process about three times or until a stable result emerges. Tell them that in the feedback stage it is up to them whether they also share the reasons for the independent estimates.

3 Disclose the correct answer, and ask the group members to compare the accuracy of their first *independent* estimates with the accuracy of the group's final result.

Possible discussion questions

- Which was more accurate: the initial independent estimates or the final group decision?

- How come the group converged in their answers?
- How is it that the group tends to be more accurate?
- What applications could this Delphi approach have during your time at college?

OVERCOMING STUDENT FEARS OF SPEAKING IN PUBLIC

Aims

- To recognize that fear of speaking in front of a group is normal and to offer suggestions for dealing with it.
- To help students cope with making presentations and to overcome early anxieties about contributing in tutorial discussions.

Procedure

1 Ask the group 'What do you believe is the most common fear among the population?'
2 Briefly note the responses on a blackboard or flipchart. Find out if there is a consensus regarding the single most common fear. Then present the list illustrated on the following page. Point out that fear of public speaking is *very* common.
3 Ask the class to suggest or brainstorm all the ways that a student faced with making a report presentation might prevent or overcome these fears. Note all the suggestions on the blackboard or flipchart so that the students have an opportunity to take notes if they choose.

Variations

Divide the group into small (five-person) groups for a brief time and ask each to generate at least five good suggestions.

Source: Newstrom and Scannell (1980).

Overcoming Student Fears of Speaking in Public: Handout

The Ten Most Common Fears (In the USA)*

1 Speaking before a group
2 Heights
3 Insects
4 Financial problems
5 Deep water
6 Sickness
7 Death
8 Flying
9 Loneliness
10 Dogs

*Wallechinsky et al (1977) *The Book of Lists,* William Morris Inc, New York.

5　Developing Learning Skills

Give a man a fish, feed him for a day. Teach a man to fish, feed him for a lifetime. (Chinese Proverb)

GOOD AND BAD LEARNING EXPERIENCES

Aims

- To identify characteristics that contribute to a good learning experience.
- To encourage students to take more responsibility for their own learning.

Procedure

1 Ask each student to recall a really good learning experience and a bad learning experience. Emphasize that this may have been in an academic context or in a non-academic context (it may be helpful to ask the class to give examples of learning in a non-academic context).

2 Ask each student to compare their experiences with those of a partner and identify what elements their good learning experiences had in common. Do the same for the bad learning experiences.

3 Ask each pair to join another pair and produce a combined list of characteristics associated with a good learning experience and with a bad learning experience. Ask a group of four to agree on a spokesperson who will report the findings of the group to the rest of the class.

4 Go round each group asking for one characteristic of a good learning experience and one characteristic of a bad learning experience; flipchart (or chalkboard) these. Continue until all of the characteristics have been listed.

Possible discussion questions

- What have the characteristics of a good learning experience got in common? And the characteristics of a bad learning experience?
- What differences in attitude make for a good learning experience? And a bad learning experience?
- Which of the identified characteristics does the student have control over and which are outside his or her control?

Variations

After the plenary, discuss in groups how each person could go about generating the characteristics of a good learning experience. Each group should flipchart its conclusions. This should be followed by a report back by each of the groups.

Materials

Flipchart paper, marker pens and bluetack.

HOW I LEARN

Aim

For individuals to identify their own patterns of learning.

Procedure

1 Identify five specific experiences where you have learned something that you enjoyed learning. Write down what they were.
2 Establish the beginning and end of each learning as if you were seeing it on film.
3 Review each one from beginning to end three times, each time discovering something new in the actual learning experience (Fill in more details – eg what you saw, said, heard, felt, did).
4 From these five examples, identify a pattern in the way you learn. What is the common sequence? Identify five steps, giving each a label.

Materials

Pen/pencil for each participant.

PATTERNS OF LEARNING

Aims

- To introduce the students to the notion that there are multiple methods by which people learn.
- To engage the students in becoming aware of which learning style they are most inclined towards.

Procedure

Explain Kolb's four learning styles or any other similar paradigm for learning. Then ask the students to assess themselves on their perceived experience and capacity to use each approach (see below).

Possible discussion questions

1 What are the strengths and weaknesses in how you learn? (Eg, with which styles are you most/least comfortable?)
2 How will your personal learning style affect your capacity to get maximum benefit from the methods used in a course of higher education?
3 What roles can your tutors play to assist your learning process?

Materials

Handout or OHP slide of the handout below (and optionally the general descriptions of learning styles following this exercise).

Source: Newstrom and Scannell (1980).

Patterns of Learning: Handout

Learning pattern self-assessment

Directions

Examine the ways that you characteristically learn new material. Assess the degree to which you feel most comfortable with each of the following methods (10 = very comfortable; 1 = least comfortable) by circling one number for each method.

A Concrete experience
(Activists prefer actual involvement in a task by doing it.)

      1   2   3   4   5   6   7   8   9   10

B Reflective observation
(Reflectors prefer to observe and think about it.)

      1   2   3   4   5   6   7   8   9   10

C Abstract conceptualization
(Theorists prefer to create integrated meaning out of seemingly independent factors defining concepts and developing models and theories.)

      1   2   3   4   5   6   7   8   9   10

D Active experimentation
(Pragmatists are keen to try out ideas, theories and techniques to see if they work in practice.)

      1   2   3   4   5   6   7   8   9   10

RECALL AND RETENTION

Aims

- To demonstrate the distinction between learning and retrieval of information.
- To help the students to find better ways of remembering.

Procedure

1 Introduce the exercise by telling the group about the power of the brain to memorize vast quantities of material. For example, 'The human brain, with its billions of cells, stores almost every "bit" of knowledge that we've ever encountered. Like a computer it is merely necessary to press the right "button" to recall items stored from years and years of experience.'

2 Tell the group that you would like to demonstrate this point about recall and retention. Ask them to relax for a moment and then ask 'Who can tell me the name of their form teacher at the age 11?' Most of the group will be able to do this. (An alternative question is to ask the group if they had a dog as a pet when they were youngsters, and what its name or physical characteristics were.)

Possible discussion questions

- When is the last time you thought about any of your teachers at the age of 11? Why would that name have 'popped' into your head so quickly? (The person was significant. The brain is phenomenal.)
- Why are some things retained while most items are so quickly forgotten?
- What can you do to more firmly implant ideas, knowledge, etc., in long-term storage? (Repeat them, recall them frequently, associate them with other items.)

Source: Adapted from Newstrom and Scannell (1980).

LIBRARY INFORMATION TRAIL

This is an example of a library exercise. It was designed to provide an introduction to one of the Brighton Polytechnic libraries (the Watts library) but it could easily be modified for any library at any academic institution. It could indeed be modified to apply to other type of facilities such as a computer centre.

Aim

To introduce the students to some of the things that they will find in the library.

Procedure

1 Ask your librarian to provide a very brief introduction to the library facilities. Then explain to your students that instead of a conventional whistle-stop tour of the library you have devised an exercise that will enable them to discover for themselves what the library contains.
2 Distribute copies of a handout similar to that below and allow enough time for students to complete the activities outlined in the handout. You may suggest that the students do the exercise in pairs or threes
3 Plenary conducted by the librarian with yourself in attendance.

Possible discussion questions

- What were the good and bad aspects of this form of introduction to the library's facilities?
- What did you find in the library that you hadn't expected? Is there anything that you would expect to find in the library that didn't seem to be there?
- Brainstorm a list of all the ways that the facilities of the library can be a useful resource in helping you to learn.

Library Information Trail: Specimen Handout

The aim of this exercise is to introduce you to some of the things that you can find and use in the Watts library.

Start your trail outside the door of the library.
On the noticeboard to the left of the door is a notice of library opening times.

1 What are the term-time opening hours?

Once inside the library, you will see a counter on your left and a flight of stairs straight ahead. To your right there are some display shelves with magazines and newspapers.

2 Name two daily newspapers taken by the library:

Now go upstairs to the main part of the library. As you go through the swing doors you will see a desk on your left and some bookshelves on your right.

Turn immediately to your right. Working your way clockwise round the library, discover the answers to the following questions:

3 What colour are the guide cards on the ends of the bays of reference books?

4 What other colour(s) are used, and what kinds of material do they indicate?

As you get to the other side of the main stairwell, there are two lots of grey filing cabinets on your right.

6 What kind of information is in these cabinets, and how is it arranged?

Continue your exploration by passing to the left of the wall and walking along the back of the library.

7 Name two of the subjects mentioned on the guide cards at the top of these bays of books:

Moving around the outside of the bookshelves you will come to an area with a collection of machinery.

8 How many computer terminals are there?

9 What are the two large machines at the end used for?

10 What is the library's new video format?

You have now covered about half of the library. As you walk through the narrow part into the second half you will see the library microfiche catalogues on your left. Look at one of the folders of the microfiche.

11 There are three different colours on the top of the microfiche sheets. What are the colours and what kinds of catalogue do they indicate?

To avoid congestion in the centre gangway, please follow the route marked on your map to the far end of the library and round the back. As you cross over to the other side of the library you will see the shelves containing the back issues of all the accounting and management journals.

12 What order are they in?

Still moving round the outside of the bookshelves to avoid congestion, you will find that after the journals there are books on these subjects. Find a title which has some copies with red tape on the spine and some with yellow tape. Look at the date labels inside the books.

13 What is the significance of the coloured tape?

When you reach the end of this block of shelves you will find a collection of videotapes. Look for those numbered between 650 and 659 on the box.

14 There is a tape about balance sheets. What is it called, and what is the number on the box?

Finally, as you turn towards the enquiry desk (where there will always be someone available to help you if you are in difficulty) you will pass three photocopiers on your left.

15 What coin do they take, and what size copies can you get for your money?

All books are borrowed and returned via the issue desk on the first floor. Go back downstairs to the counter area and have a look at the various notices that you can see.

16 What kinds of material do we charge fines on?

17 What is the maximum fine?

18 Can you renew your books when they are due back?

19 What colour card should you fill in if you want to reserve a book?

20 Above the security gates there is a final notice. What does it say?

WATTS BUILDING LIBRARY PLAN

 C Catalogues
CA Calculators
CE CEEFAX/ORACLE
CO Computers
 E Enquiry Desk
 M Microfilm Readers
 P Photocopiers and
    Change Machine
PR PRESTEL
 T Typewriters
 V Videotape Carrels
 A Audiotape Carrels
CH Change Machine
CR Company Reports

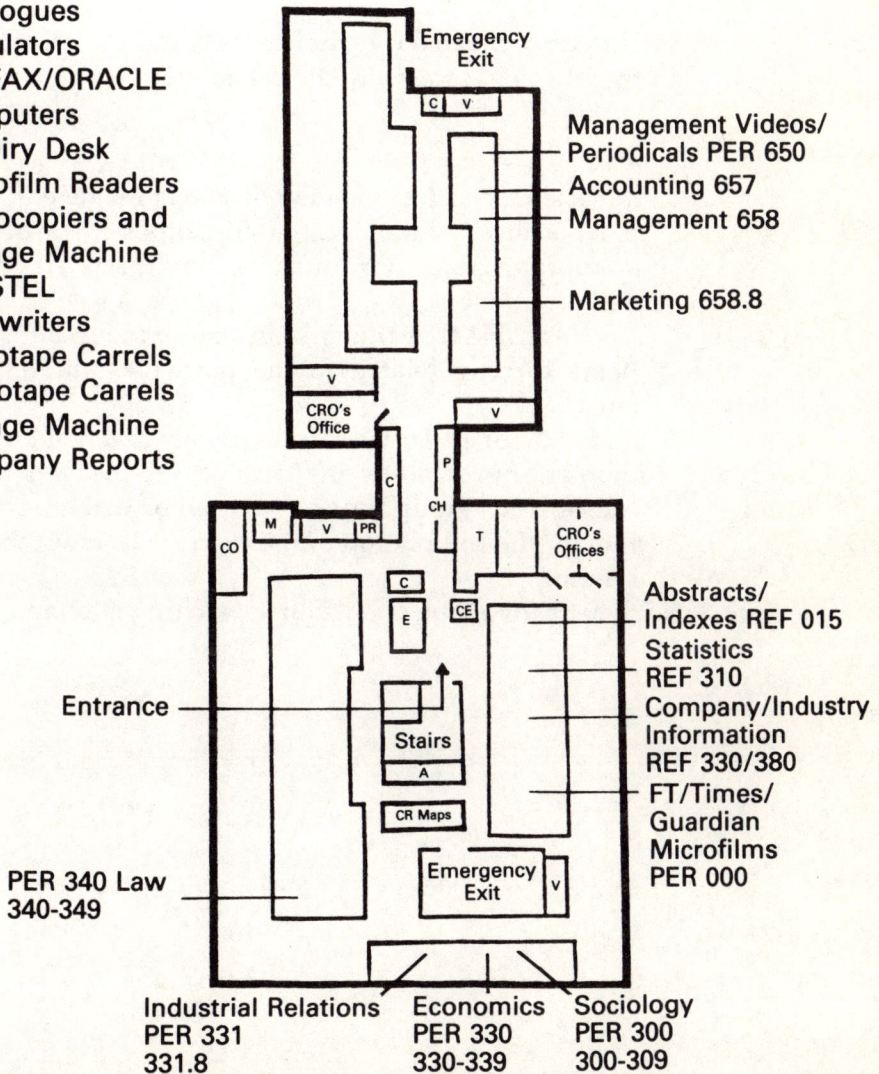

Emergency Exit

Management Videos/
Periodicals PER 650
Accounting 657
Management 658

Marketing 658.8

CRO's Office

CRO's Offices

Abstracts/
Indexes REF 015
Statistics
REF 310
Company/Industry
Information
REF 330/380
FT/Times/
Guardian
Microfilms
PER 000

Entrance

Stairs

CR Maps

Emergency Exit

PER 340 Law
340-349

Industrial Relations
PER 331
331.8

Economics
PER 330
330-339

Sociology
PER 300
300-309

LIBRARY FAMILIARIZATION

This exercise illustrates an activity-based approach to library induction. It was originally designed for students on a personnel management course. It is important that this sort of exercise is tailored to the interests of the students involved. Like the previous activity (Library Information Trail) it is included as a model to help readers to design their own exercises tailored to the library needs of their own students.

Aim

To introduce the major reference tools and sources of information in the library – especially the catalogue.

Procedure

1 This exercise is designed to *follow* a more general introduction to the facilities of the library (with either a whistle-stop tour or an appropriate activity such as the Library Information Trail exercise above).
2 It is desirable that this 'library familiarization' exercise has a theme directly related to the particular studies of the students.
3 Students can either work individually and hand in the exercise for marking or work in pairs or groups and present their findings as a group report – written or verbal. An appropriate time for the completion of the exercise is about the third week of term.
4 Plenary involving both course teaching staff and librarian.

Library Familiarization: Specimen Handout

This exercise is designed to help you to find information in the Watts library. The most important tool in the library is the catalogue.

1 The *name* microfiche with the orange stripes across the top lists all library materials alphabetically under the author and the title. Use this to look up the book by *P MARGINSON* on industrial relations published in 1986.

    ● What is the full title?
    ● What is the library class number?

2 If you need information on a particular subject you should use the *subject index* in the blue binders. Find the classification number for the management aspects of *industrial relations.*

You may need to use the *dictionaries* or *encyclopedias* in the reference section to help you to understand the technical terms.

3 Use the microfiche catalogue to find the class number for the *Encyclopedia of Personnel Management.* According to the encyclopedia, what kinds of topics may be covered in *personnel policy?*

An essential part of research into any topic involves locating articles in journals and newspapers, and in making use of statistical data.

4 The *Employment Gazette* for June 1987 contains an article on the importance of training managers. Which two key areas of management are identified as being in particular need of more training?

5 Training for managers indicates the value of education for efficiency. It has also been suggested that education is linked to productivity. Find *Research Index Industries Amalgamation* (ref: 016.33) for 1986. An article in the *British Journal of Industrial Relations* compares the situation in Great Britain with that in the United States. What does the author of the article conclude to be the most striking contrast between the two countries?

6   Another important aspect is that of managing labour relations. A useful source of articles of this kind of topic is *Anbar* (ref: 016.658). By looking under *personnel* (section 3.47) in vol. 15 find an article by P K Edwards. What conclusions does he draw?

7   Recent developments in relations between management and unions have included *no-strike agreements. British Humanities Index* (ref: 016.3) for 1986 indexes an article under the *Industrial Relations: Great Britain* heading about a no-strike deal in action. Which company is involved?

8   Industrial disputes have always had a detrimental effect on productivity. *Social Trends* for 1987 gives figures for the number of days lost due to stoppages in 1984 and 1985. Approximately how many days were lost each year?

9   Research has suggested a rather different solution to improving labour efficiency. Find the *Times Index* for 1986 and discover what the solution is! When did the article appear in the newspaper?

10 Problems between management and staff sometimes require an outside arbitrator. The *Times Union Handbook* gives the address for the South East Region Office of ACAS. What is it?

11 Most disputes arise over pay and conditions. It is sometimes helpful to know the average wages being paid to full-time male workers doing similar work in other areas. From the *New Earnings Survey* discover the most recent figure for the car industry. How different is the figure for women?

12 Finally, if you have time, and you feel like a little light relief, you might like to find and watch the videotape called *Managing Staff.* Does it give you any food for thought?

WRITING

It is when students are being *active* and *constructive* in their learning that their purposes and their conception of the whole intellectual enterprise they are involved in becomes most apparent. This is especially evident when they are engaged in writing.

Students understand what essays are for in very different ways. They are trying to achieve very different sorts of things when they set out to write essays. They have different *intentions* when they write. This is a hard notion to explain to students in the abstract, but very easy if concrete examples can be given to illustrate what sort of written outcomes result from different intentions. It is possible to carefully choose pairs of students' essays to illustrate the particular differences in intentions that you are concerned with – or even write your own.

The pair of short essays offered here as 'materials' have been written in strikingly different ways. Although both the students who wrote them attempt to answer the same questions, their essays embody quite different notions of the nature of the task of essay writing. Two sorts of somewhat distinct factors may be involved in these different notions. First, there may be differences in the conceptions of learning in general which underlie the students' intentions. Second, there may be differences in the way these students understood the specific assessment requirements of the course that they were studying.

Wherever this pair of essays has been used by a group of academics it has led to disagreements about which is best. They disagree about what assessment systems should be measuring. Both of these sorts of issues (about the goals of learning and about the criteria of assessment) are raised by this exercise. Because the variety of issues raised can be so broad it may be helpful, if the size of your student group permits it, to lead the pooling of points on the plenary into a general discussion of the purpose of essay writing.

Aims

- To help students to reconceptualize their learning and reorient them towards new learning goals.
- To help students appreciate *explicitly* the criteria that they apply *implicitly* when writing essays.

dure

1 Distribute copies of the two essays on noise pollution problems caused by Concorde (shown on the following pages).
2 Give the students the following instructions:

Working alone (20 minutes)
Read through these two students' answers to the question. Which answer is best, and why?
Working in pairs (10 minutes)
Compare your comments. Which answer is best, and why?
Working in fours (15 minutes)
Pool your conclusions. Were these students trying to do the same thing? Describe what you think each was trying to do.
Working in plenary (15 minutes)
I'd like each group in turn to make a comment about one of the answers, and about what the student was aiming to do.

3 Lead into a general discussion.

Possible discussion questions

- What conclusions can you draw from this exercise about the purposes of higher education?
- How are the criteria of assessment likely to differ for different subjects?
- How could you find out what criteria a particular member of staff is applying when marking your essays?

Source: Gibbs (1981).

Writing Exercise: Handout

Assess the noise pollution problems caused by Concorde around airports.

Answer 1

The sound limit at Kennedy airport, New York, is 112 PNdB (PNdB means perceived noise decibels – a logarithmic scale of noise), and at Heathrow, London, 110 PNdB. The manufacturers of Concorde (Sud-Aviation and the British Aircraft Corporation) have promised that Concorde will range between 104 and 108 PNdB, depending on its weight at take-off.

At the start of Concorde operations at Heathrow, 21 of the first 35 departures exceeded 110 PNdB, and in the first eight months of operation 97 departures exceeded 110 PNdB. Overall in 1976 there were 109 infringements of Heathrow's limit by Concorde. These measurements of Concorde were about 7 PNdB lower than during its early endurance trials. At the same time there were 1,841 infringements by subsonic jets. Concorde rarely features in the list of the ten noisiest take-offs each month at Heathrow, and subsonic aircraft at Kennedy have been recorded at 221 PNdB – twice the limit.

At Dulles Airport, Washington, Concorde has averaged 119.9 PNdB on landing. This is 12–13 PNdB higher than the average for subsonic aircraft. The noise levels have been going down, and with them the number of complaints. In September 1976 the average level was 121.3 PNdB and there were 186 complaints (29 of these to one takeoff). In October the average was 117.4 PNdB and there were 101 complaints. During this time polls of opinion concerning Concorde's trial period at Dulles showed an initial opposition of 36.9% drop to 26.2%. In New York opposition to Concorde landing at Kennedy has dropped from 63% in January 1976 to 53% in April 1977.

While 500,000 people are affected by aircraft noise in Washington, 2,000,000 are affected at Kennedy. It has been estimated that 400,000 extra people will be affected by noise if 80 Concordes serve 12 US cities. This represents a 1% increase. Bumps in the runway at Kennedy force Concorde to take off closer to heavily populated areas, but due to advanced flight-control characteristics Concorde can begin to bank at an altitude of 100 ft compared with an average of 480 ft for subsonic aircraft, and so can turn away from heavily populated areas sooner after take-off.

Answer 2

Opposition to Concorde based on noise pollution takes two main themes. The first is concerned with the 'sonic boom' – a phenomenon of supersonic flight unique to Concorde amongst commercial aircraft. The second is concerned with noise levels around airports caused during take-off and landing. This second theme is common to all aircraft, and the issue at stake is whether Concorde is significantly noisier than subsonic aircraft.

Comparisons with other aircraft are complicated by the changing nature of jet fleets. Early jet aircraft (eg the DC8 and 707) use turbo-jet engines, and whilst these have been quietened, they are much noisier than second-generation fan-jet engine aircraft (eg DC10 and jumbo 747). Eventually these older aircraft will be phased out, but at the moment Concorde is being compared with them.

There are also problems of measurement. Objective measures (meters giving a reading in decibels) cannot give any impression of 'shrillness' or subjectively experienced nuisance. An aircraft giving higher decibel readings may not be experienced as 'noisier' by someone hearing it take off. Subjective measures also involve problems, as 'noise' is such a multi-faceted phenomenon, and different people use different criteria in assessing it. There are dangers, also, in questionnaire surveys of reactions of people living around airports. Average ratings of 'nuisance' change over time without any changes in objectively measured decibel levels or frequency of aircraft movements, and so other factors must be involved. These factors can be political. Boeing took care to contract for parts for its SST at factories surrounding Kennedy airport, so that votes concerning whether SSTs should be allowed to use the airport would be influenced by residents' concerns for their jobs! Workers at Filton and Toulouse would hardly try to ban Concorde landing near their homes, however noisy it is!

Finally there is a variation in recorded noise levels dependent on the skill of the pilot, and load factors of the aircraft. Subsonic aircraft have been measured at twice the legal noise level, struggling to take off with heavy loads in adverse conditions. Concorde has been flying underloaded, with skilled pilots, who have even been reported banking away from noise monitors.

Given this variety of problems it would seem likely that Concorde causes even more noise pollution than data suggests, and that in comparison with subsonic jets it will become comparatively worse as time goes on.

HOLDING THE RULER:
Communication and Group Skills

Aims

- To improve listening skills.
- To develop understanding of communication patterns in a group.

Procedure

1 Divide the course members into groups of about seven people.
2 Explain that this activity will take the form of a discussion with a special rule. The 'special rule' is that 'possession of a particular object will determine who speaks'. Choose something convenient like a ruler to be the 'particular object'. The person with the 'object' must keep it until another person indicates non-verbally that they wish to have it. The person with the ruler can refuse to give it to the person requesting it.
3 Provide a topic for the group to discuss. (There's a list of possible topics at the end of the activity titled 'Active Listening and Communication Skills' – see the index). Alternatively, provide a topic based on the experiences or aims of the group. It's important to choose a topic that will produce significant interaction. You may want to quickly brainstorm topics to find one that generates sufficient energy.
4 Give participants the opportunity to prepare for the dicussion by making some notes first. This tends to heighten participation.
5 Hand the ruler to one member of the group.
6 Allow discussion to continue for as long as it is useful (10-15 minutes is a reasonable time).
7 Possible discussion questions for plenary:
   - What actually happened?
   - How did you feel while it was happening?
   - How did 'the rule' affect the discussion?
   - How different was that from a 'normal' group discussion?
   - How do you feel about it now?
   - What did you learn from doing it?
   - How would you like to behave differently next time?
   - How can you use this experience to improve your group work?

Materials

A convenient object such as a ruler (or pen).

Variations

- The ruler is passed round the group from hand to hand, conveying an invitation – though not a compulsion – for everyone to contribute.
- An observer outside of the discussion group can make a record of the interactions within the group. One way to do this is to draw a symbol for each of the participants in their relative positions and then draw a line to indicate each passage of the ruler.
- Another way to record the pattern of communication within the group is to replace the ruler by a ball of string which is to be passed round, unwinding with each interaction.
- This activity can be combined with the 'fishbowl feedback' activity (see index).

DEVELOPING GROUP SKILLS

This is an exercise for the students after they have had some experience of working together in groups.

Aim

To give students an opportunity to reflect upon how they can contribute as group members to more successful group outcomes.

Procedure

1 Ask each student to identify from *their own experience* one quality, attitude or other contribution that a person can bring to a group that will make it more effective – and write this down on a piece of paper. Don't ask the students to put their names on their contributions.
2 The tutor collects the pieces of paper and writes them on the blackboard or flipchart and uses this to stimulate a discussion about what makes some groups more effective than others.
3 Ask students to identify the opposite of each of the qualities and attitudes on the board or flipchart and record these on the board/chart also. If a positive quality/attitude generates several

opposites then record all of them. Use this material for a brief discussion about ineffective groups.

4 End the session by summarizing what has been written on the board/chart:

'So a group is likely to be really effective if its members contribute: . . . '

'And a group is likely to be a real disaster if these are what its members bring: . . . '

FIRST CLASS ANSWER

Very poor answers to essay questions give the impression that the student was following a set of instructions such as:

'Write down whatever you can think of about this topic, in the order in which you remember things. Do not give your answer a logical structure. Include material that is not relevant to the question asked if you can't think of anything better. Do not use your critical faculties. Do not attempt to draw conclusions.'

It is possible to rewrite an essay question in the form in which students with different quality answers appear to have understood it.

Aim

To give students the opportunity to compare different approaches to answering essay questions.

Procedure

1 Give students copies of the First Class Answer Handout and a question from last year's exam paper. Ask them to rewrite the question in the same way as the one on the handout. Get them to try individually for five minutes and then work in groups of three for another five minutes to produce a joint version.

2 Ask the groups of three to read out their versions.

3 If students find this either very difficult or very enjoyable, you can run through the process again with a second question.

Source: Habeshaw, Habeshaw and Gibbs (1987).

First Class Answer: Handout

Essay question

This is a question from an examination paper on the psychology of child development.

Compare and contrast the consequences of blindness and deafness for language development.

This is how students who gained different degree classifications seem to have interpreted the question.

First class

'Identify the consequences of blindness and deafness for language development. Compare and contrast these consequences, drawing conclusions about the nature of language development.'

Upper second class

'Identify the consequences of blindness and deafness for language development. Compare and contrast these consequences.'

Lower second class

'List some of the features of blindness and deafness. List some consequences for development including a few for language development.'

Third class

'Write down almost anything that you can think of about blindness, deafness, child development and language development. Do not attempt to draw any justified conclusions.'

6   **Empowering Students**

In the ongoing flux of life, human beings may undergo many changes. Arriving, departing, growing, declining, achieving, failing – every change involves a loss and a gain. The old environment must be given up, the new accepted. People come and go; one job is lost, another begun; territory and possessions are acquired or sold; new skills are learnt and old abandoned; expectations are fulfilled or hopes dashed – in all these situations individuals are faced with the need to give up one mode of life and accept another. (Parkes, 1975)

POSITIVE SELF-CONCEPT

Aim

To demonstrate that it *is* acceptable to verbalize one's own positive qualities.

Procedure

1 Ask the group to divide into pairs.
2 Each person is then asked to write four or five things that they really like about themselves. (NB Since most people tend to be modest and hesitant to write something nice about themselves, some light encouragement on the facilitator's part may be needed. For example, 'enthusiastic', 'intelligent', 'diligent', 'honest', 'trusting'.)
3 After three or four minutes have passed, ask each person to share with their respective partners the items that they wrote down.

Possible discussion questions

- Did you feel uncomfortable with this activity? If so, why?
- Were you honest with yourself – did you hold back on your positive qualities?
- What reaction did you get from your partner when you disclosed your strengths? (Eg, surprise, encouragement, reinforcement?)

Source: Newstrom and Scannell (1980).

GETTING FEEDBACK

Aims

- To help the students to appreciate the roles of feedback in the learning process.
- To identify sources of feedback.
- To develop skills in receiving feedback.

Procedure

1 Ask the students what is meant by the term 'feedback'? Ask for some examples. Make sure that both positive and negative feedback are referred to and that the distinction is clear.
2 Brainstorm answers to the question, 'In what ways is feedback useful?'

   Summarize the results of the brainstorm by noting the very general role of feedback in the learning process. Conclude this section with a statement along the following lines:

'If we can increase the amount of feedback that we receive then we will learn more. We will receive more feedback if we are skilled at generating it and good at receiving it.'

3 Ask students to consider the following question individually: 'What possible sources of feedback do we have?'
4 Form pairs to compare answers and then consider, 'How can we generate more feedback?'
5 Combine pairs to produce groups of four to compare answers to the previous question and then consider, 'What impediments are there to receiving feedback?'
6 Each group of four joins another group of four and the resulting groups of eight consider, 'What can we do to be good at receiving feedback?'
7 Plenary focused on bringing together the ideas generated by each of the questions.

Possible discussion questions

- Why are we reluctant to give people positive feedback? (We take their skills and virtues for granted. We are embarrassed. We are worried that they will become conceited.)
- Why are we reluctant to give people negative feedback? (Will the person be upset and if so can we cope with this? Will it

damage the relationship that we have with the person? Will they really understand that we are trying to be helpful and supportive or will they receive the feedback as criticism and become defensive?)
- Which do you find easiest – giving or receiving feedback?
- When is a good time to seek (or to give) feedback?
- Where is a good place to seek (or to give) feedback?

TIME MANAGEMENT

Aims

- To enable students to manage their time better.
- To help them to prepare for the demands on their time that the increasing complexity of the course makes.
- To help them to prepare for the future, when they will be responsible for managing their own time and work.

Procedure

Give the students the following three tasks:

1 *Objectives.* Write down your objectives for yourself as a student. For example, what do you want in relation to your academic work? Do you want a good or excellent result, or are you aiming just to scrape through? Are you mainly concerned with formal course results, or do you also want to develop significantly personally? What do you want in your social life? And so on.

   It is important that you clarify these objectives before you go on to the next task. When you are clear about your personal values and priorities, it will be much easier to manage everything else.

2 *Time plan.* Make a time plan for two weeks (specify dates). Show mornings, afternoons and evenings, and include weekends; show how you are going to use these periods. Include leisure activities and any paid work as well as work on your course of study.

   If you prefer a more flexible approach than this to managing your time, then describe that instead, and justify it.

3 *Tutorial.* Come to a tutorial (specify a time halfway through the two-week period) to monitor how well you are doing on the task so far, and to help you manage your time even more

effectively the following week. Be sure to bring your objectives and time plan to the tutorial.

ACTIVE LISTENING AND COMMUNICATION SKILLS

Aims

- To identify hindrances to effective listening.
- To develop active listening skills.

Procedure

1 Briefly outline the goals of the activity.
2 Form triads (groups of three). The members of each triad **to** name themselves as either A, B or C.
3 Distribute copies of the Possible Discussion Topics sheet.
4 Give the following instructions:

   a) A selects a topic and speaks first
   B is the listener in the first round.
   C is the referee in the first round.
   b) The role of the referee is to ensure that the listener doesn't distort, omit, add to, respond to, or interpret what the speaker said.
   c) the selected topic is discussed by the speaker. As speaker, try to be aware of the listener's ability to understand what you are saying.
   d) The listener paraphrases (gives a summary in his/her own words) without notes.
   e) If either the speaker or referee think that the summary is incorrect in any way then they are free to interject to make corrections.
   f) The time for the whole process of speaking and summarising in each round is seven minutes.

5 At the end of the first round (after seven minutes) respond to procedural questions.
6 Repeat the process twice as each member of the group takes a turn to be A, B **and** C.
7 Distribute copies of the Questions for Discussion sheet which the triads use as a basis for discussing the experience. After

this, elicit ideas about barriers to effective listening from the entire group.

Variations

- Generate topics for discussion within the group: 'What are some topics about which there is likely to be disagreement within this group? Post suggestions for use in the exercise.
- You could offer a list of more relevant (but probably less contentious) topics including such items as: 'the main differences between school and college', 'the value of groupwork as a means of learning', 'what I can do to get the most out of this course?', 'what I want to get out of this course in addition to passing the examinations', 'my concerns and fears about this course' etc.
- If two participants do not seem to be speaking and/or listening effectively to each other you can ask the entire group to referee.
- You can change the 'rules' so that in the first round the listener 'parrots' the speaker, word-for-word, in the next round the listener paraphrases, and in the third round the listener reflects the *feelings* being expressed by the speaker. If you do the above then have a final round incorporating all three listening modes.

Materials

'Possible Discussion Topics' and 'Questions for Discussion' sheets for each course member.

Active Listening and Communication Skills: Possible Discussion Topics Handout

1 Unilateral nuclear disarmament

2 The women's movement

3 Socialism

4 The present government's political record

5 How best to deal with dangerous dogs

6 Capital punishment

7 Prison reform

8 Drug use and abuse

9 How to reduce unemployment

10 The harmful effects of pornography

11 Legalising prostitution

12 The best way to reduce inflation

13 The best way to reduce environmental pollution

14 Making *all* public areas no-smoking areas

15 Random police drink tests on drivers

16 Closing of all public house car parks as a solution to the problem of drinking and driving

17 How best to deal with convicted terrorists

18 Reducing car pollution by raising the cost of petrol

Active Listening and Communication Skills: Questions for Discussion Handout

1 How did you feel in each of the three roles (speaker, listener and referee)?

2 Which of the three roles did you find easiest? What difficulties did you experience in the other two roles?

3 What hindrances to effective listening emerged during the activity?

4 What did you find out about how succesful you are in expressing yourself?

5 How can you apply what you have learned from this activity? What risks might there be in acting on what you've just learned?

6 What applications might you make of the paraphrasing technique?

SKILLS AUCTION

Aims

- To encourage students to engage in self-assessment.
- To help them acquire new skills.
- To foster an atmosphere of trust.

Procedure

1 Ask the students to write (anonymously) one skill that they would like to have to be more successful (academically or in any other way) on the course. Examples might be:

- I would like to be better at taking exams.
- I would like to be able to make friends more quickly.
- I would like to be able to remember people's names.

2 Put all the papers in a hat.
3 Someone reads out all the papers, and someone else writes them on a flipchart or chalkboard.
4 Everyone is given a notional £100 to spend at the auction. Each person is responsible for keeping track of his or her own bidding.
5 Someone acts as auctioneer, and the auction is held. Each person can bid for as many skills as they want until they have spent their £100. When the skill has been sold, the new owner keeps the piece of paper.
6 Discussion in groups about how each person could go about acquiring the skill that they have 'bought'.
7 Plenary.

Materials

Flipchart or chalkboard, hat and gavel (optional).

Source: Brandes and Ginnis (1986).

BRAINSTORMING

Aims

- To generate a large number of useful ideas on any subject or problem by suspending criticism, judgement and evaluation.
- To develop groupwork skills by introducing a group technique for creative problem-solving.
- To encourage cooperative and collaborative behaviour.

Procedure

1 The facilitator says, 'Imagine that you are cast ashore on a desert island, naked and with only one man-made object: a belt. Using your wildest imaginations think of as many uses as possible for the belt.' State the following rules:

- No comment, criticism, judgement or evaluation during the brainstorming phase.
- As many ideas as possible – the objective is *quantity* not quality.
- Wildest ideas possible.
- Build upon each others' ideas.

2 The facilitator writes down *every* idea on a flipchart, chalkboard or a sheet of newsprint, without comment, discarding nothing. The facilitator can also put in ideas (thus becoming a contributing member of the group).

3 After the ideas have stopped coming (this can be checked by doing a 'round' – see the second variation below) the facilitator points to each and asks how many people think it has possibilities. The ones that have no votes at all are deleted. The remaining ones are discussed in detail, and eventually a 'best one' is chosen (by acclaim or by voting).

4 The facilitator forms groups of about six participants each. Each group selects a secretary to record the ideas. The groups are then given three minutes to brainstorm uses of a cola bottle on a desert island (instead of a belt).

5 The facilitator leads a discussion of brainstorming as an approach to creative problem-solving.

Variations

- Other objects can be used in the problem such as a rope, a shoe, an oar, an economics textbook, a brick, etc.

- Instead of allowing students to call out ideas ('free-for-all') an alternative procedure is to use 'rounds'. In a 'round' each person in the group contributes an idea or says 'pass'. Or the two approaches can be combined: start off with a free-for-all and when the flow of ideas becomes thin do a few rounds to finish.

- In stage 4 (above) the total number of ideas counted after the ideas-generating phase and the total for each group is announced. The teams are then given a few minutes to reach a group decision about which are their five most original ideas (ie ones that the other teams will not have). Each team then reads out the five that they have chosen. Points are given for any ideas which have not been thought of by any other team.

- This exercise may be done as a preliminary to a problem-solving session involving a 'real' problem (see Handout for some suggestions).

Possible discussion questions

- How could two or more of the ideas generated be used in combination?
- In this exercise a large amount of creativity was released by suspending criticism, evaluation or judgement – so what is the role of criticism, evaluation and judgement in the problem-solving?
- What conditions are favourable to creativity? (In what conditions/situations do you feel most creative?)

Materials

Marker pens and flipchart paper or sheets of newsprint.

Suggestions for Induction Topics to Brainstorm: Handout

1 Activities to do during your period at college when you are not studying.

2 Activities to help you learn in addition to attending classes or reading.

3 How to cope with a bad lecturer.

4 How do you know when you've done something well? (ie what possible sources of feedback can you think of?)

5 Possible problems of transition into higher education.

6 Good aspects of transition into higher education.

7 Bad aspects of transition into higher education.

8 What makes an effective member of a group?

9 What is it that makes a 'supportive' group supportive?

10 Improvements to the induction programme for next year.

11 Reasons for choosing this as a place to study.

12 Possible difficulties in adjusting to studying at this institution.

13 What constitutes a good 'climate' for learning?

14 What new skills would be helpful for living and studying here?

15 What sources of stress could be encountered in the transition into higher education?

16 What to do when the book that you have been recommended is not in the library.

17 'Some people seem to thrive on transitions, others crumble beneath them; some people develop and grow from crises while others become demoralized and slide. We are beginning to discover that as with everything else there are skills for coping effectively with the transitions, and that some people are better endowed than others.' (Hopson and Scally – 1980).

What skills and attitudes are helpful in coping with transitions and making the most of the opportunities for development and growth that transitions provide?

18 The transition into higher education, like other transitions, involves taking on new things and 'letting go' of others. What things might it involve letting go of?

19 What makes a good seminar?

20 What makes a 'good' tutor?

21 What makes a 'bad' tutor?

22 What are tutors really like?

23 What makes a 'good' student?

24 What makes a 'bad' student?

25 What are students really like?

26 What makes for enjoyable learning?

27 What study skills would it be good to have?

28 Suppose that you are dissatisfied with your skills in taking notes in lectures and you feel that you need some help with this. What resources are available to you?

29 When you are working on a group assignment, how can you tell if your group is not working well?

30 How do you know when you are learning effectively?

FISHBOWL FEEDBACK

Aims

- To develop skills in giving and receiving feedback.
- To develop awareness of group processes.

Procedure

1 This activity involves two groups of from five to twelve participants. Ask the course members to seat themselves in two circles as follows:

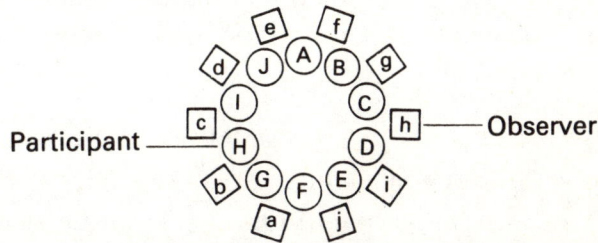

Participant ——— ⬜c ⬜h ——— Observer

2 The inner-circle group engages in an activity chosen by the facilitator (eg a discussion of some relevant topic such as the expected differences between school and college).

3 Ask the members of the outer circle to observe the effects of individuals on both the group process and the accomplishment of the task.

4 After ten minutes ask the observers to give feedback to the members of the inner circle. (Optional: ask the observers to give their feedback in accordance with the 'criteria for effective feedback' handout).

5 Repeat the process such that the observers now become inner-circle participants.

6 Introduce another activity and repeat both stages. A possible second activity is given in the exercise titled *'Holding the Ruler: Developing Group Skills'* (see index) – this is a discussion such that group members can only speak when they are holding a specified object such as a ruler.

7 Reassemble the whole group and discuss the process and its lessons.

Variations

- A co-facilitator briefs observers in a separate room on specific things to look for (such as extent of contribution, nature of contribution, behaviour when not speaking, etc).
- More than one pair of groups may be directed simultaneously.

Fishbowl Feedback: Effective Feedback Handout

Feedback is more effective if:

- *It is descriptive rather than evaluative.* It is more useful to say: 'Your tone of voice when you presented your report to the rest of the class made me feel that you were really interested in the subject' than to say: 'That was a good presentation.'

- *It is specific rather than general.* It is more useful to say: 'You interrupted someone else on at least three occasions during that discussion' than to say: 'You were a real pain in the neck during that discussion.'

- *It is directed towards behaviour that can be changed.* It is more useful to say: 'I would like it better if you would look at me when you speak to me' than to say: 'You're insensitive just like all men.'

- *It focuses on behaviour rather than the person.* It is more useful to say: 'I feel angry that you contributed so little to this group project' than to say: 'You're lazy and a liability in this group.'

- *It is owned by the giver.* It is more useful to say: 'I feel irritated when you interrupt other members of the group when they are speaking' than to say: 'You talk too much in this group.'

- *It is given as soon as possible after the behaviour to which it refers.*

- *It is checked to ensure clear communication.*

- *It offers alternatives wherever possible.*

- *It is solicited rather than imposed.* When feedback is asked for there is less likelihood that it will be received as criticism.

- *The feedback is given to the person who owns the behaviour* rather than to a third party.

7   Making the Most of the Transition

We are not unlike a particularly hardy crustacean. The lobster grows by developing and shedding a series of hard, protective shells. Each time it expands from within, the confining shell must be sloughed off. It is left exposed and vulnerable until, in time, a new covering grows to replace the old.

With each passage from one stage of human growth to the next we too must shed a protective structure. We are left exposed and vulnerable but also yeasty and embryonic again, capable of stretching in ways we hadn't known before. (Sheehy 1977)

A STORY FOR TRANSITIONS

Aims

- To help the students explore their own judgments, assumptions and values.
- To stimulate the students to consider the extent to which they create their own reality.

Procedure

1 Read the following story aloud:

There was once an old man sitting against a large tree, by the side of the road, gazing off into the middle distance, and contemplating . . . who knows what? Along came a stranger who stopped to eat his lunch and pass the time of day. In the course of the conversation, the stranger pointed to the village nestled in the valley below, and asked, 'What are the people like in the town down there? I'm just moving there you know.'

The old man thought for a moment, then threw the question back 'What were they like in the town where you used to live, my friend?'

A thundercloud seemed to pass across the face of the stranger: 'Oh, they were a terrible lot. Liars, cheats and really selfish – most of them only cared about themselves. And they never had a kind word for anyone.'

The old man shook his head and spoke, 'Well, that's what the people are like in the village down there, my son.'

The stranger heaved himself to his feet and walked sadly down the hill. The old man leaned back against the tree and fell asleep.

Later, when he awoke, he saw another stranger approaching. The newcomer smiled, and asked if he could share the shade of the tree. The old man shifted over to make room for him, and gratefully accepted the stranger's offer of an apple and some cheese.

As they chatted, the stranger pointed to village in the valley: 'What are the people like in that village?' he asked. 'I'm thinking of moving there soon.'

Once again the old man parried the question, 'What were they like where you've just come from, my son?'

The stranger's face lit up. 'Oh, they were great people, the salt of the earth. I never heard a harsh word from them or saw an unkind act while I was there. I only wish that I could stay but it's time to move on.

The old man smiled with pleasure and responded: 'Well, I'm pleased to say that that is exactly how you'll find those people in the village below.'

2 In small groups, ask the students to discuss the meaning of the story and write a moral (or morals) for it.
3 Write all the possible meanings and morals on the flipchart or board.
4 Discuss, with reference to transition to higher education.

Possible discussion questions

- What opportunities are provided by the move to higher education for changing the ways that you experience the world?
- In what different ways do we 'create our own experience?'

Materials

Flipchart and pen (or board and chalk).

Source: Brandes and Ginnis (1986).

A QUESTION OF ATTITUDES

Aim

To help the students explore how their own attitudes affect the quality of their experiences.

Procedure

1 Ask the students to write down one word to describe this person: 'Jane does things by herself, spends most of her time alone, and doesn't do much with other people.'
2 Then ask the students whether the word that they wrote down was positive or negative. Some will have written words like 'lonely' or 'unhappy'. Others will have written positive words like 'self-reliant'.
3 Repeat with some other illustrations. For example, give one word for 'a life in which nothing much changes' (boring? or peaceful?). And another for 'not having one set of circumstances within which to operate' (freedom? or insecurity?).

Possible discussion questions

1 What's the difference between a 'problem' and a 'challenge'?
2 What attitudes could help you to get more out of your course of higher education?

ARM-FOLDING EXERCISE

Aims

- To demonstrate our innate resistance to change or being changed.
- To raise awareness of the opportunities for change afforded by the transition into higher education.

Procedure

Ask the group to fold their arms in front of them. Tell them that they should *not* glance down to identify which arm rests on top of the other. Then ask them to quickly unfold their arms and refold them in the *opposite* way (i.e., if the left arm was initially on top, it should now be underneath the right arm).

Possible discussion questions

- Why did you feel this awkward? (It was a change from years of old habits.)
- How does it feel in the new position? (Uncomfortable.)
- If even this slight physical change may have some built-in resistance, what implications does this have for more substantial physical or intellectual change?

Source: Newstrom and Scannell (1980).

I LIKE YOU – YOU'RE DIFFERENT

Aims

- To encourage students to feel proud of their differences rather than feeling the need to be conformists.
- To encourage an open attitude toward others and their differences.

Procedure

1 Before giving the assignment, introduce the activity as follows:

'Very often we feel that it's important to be like other people, and we worry if we feel that we're different. At times it's fine to be like others, but it's also important to accept and be proud of our differences. There are many ways that we are like each other in this class, but there are also things about us that are not true of anyone else in this class.

'For tomorrow write down on a card three things you feel good about that make you different from anyone else in this class. That is, they may not be true of anyone else here.'

2 Give three examples from your own life to show what you mean. Be imaginative and humorous, if possible, to set the example for others to do so.
3 Distribute cards and tell the students to write their names on the cards that they turn in and not to tell anyone what they wrote. Announce that you will collect the cards and read them aloud, and that they will guess the identity of the people.
4 Before starting the activity the next time, reiterate the positive aspects of being different. Then read each card aloud, asking for guesses as to who each one is. Based on the names guessed

per card, have the class vote on whose card it is. Then announce who the correct person is. If the right person is not among those named, after the vote ask them to keep guessing, continue until the correct person is found. Include a card for yourself also, and don't make your differences so obvious that they will know that it is you.

5 When all the cards have been read and the identities guessed, ask questions to get students to recall the information on them: 'Who remembers something different about someone in the class?' The students can then make statements such as 'Barbara lived in Chile' or 'Bob won an art contest'.

6 After a number of these statements have been made, have the students ask questions of the class based on the cards: 'Who has climbed a mountain in the Alps?' 'Who is the oldest of seven children?' 'Who once ate seven cartons of yoghurt for a bet?'

7 Ask the students how they felt about this activity and what they learned from doing it. You can conclude the discussion by summarizing:

'Sometimes we feel uneasy because we believe we're different. Other times we feel discouraged when we think that there's not much that sets us off as being different from others. Often people are interested in us *because* of our differences. We've just learned a number of new and interesting things about those in our class that probably makes us want to know even more about them.

Hopefully, we enjoyed sharing our differences, hearing others impressed by them, and now we can probably think of many more ways in which we are different and proud of it.'

Materials

A card to be filled out by every student.

LIFELINES

Aim

For students to reflect upon and learn from their experiences.

Procedure

Instructions for the students:

1 Take a very large sheet of paper and draw a graph with the horizontal axis representing your life in years to date and the vertical axis being a subjective scale to indicate peaks and troughs in your life's experiences.

2 On the graph plot two lines: First, your experiences of success and its loss or absence. Second, your experiences of fulfilment and its loss or absence.

An example graph is given here.

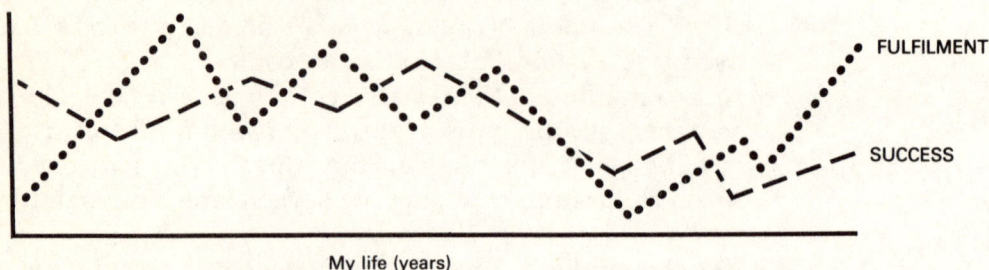

My life (years)

3 On your graph make notes and/or draw simple appropriate illustrations at different stages of these lifelines, particularly at the peaks and troughs. Take as much time as you like to do this – *Remember, this is your life!*

4 Reflect on your distinctive pattern of experience. The handout may help you to focus on particular aspects of your experience.

5 Create a sentence or statement that for you summarizes your distinctive pattern of experience.

6 Split into groups of twos or threes to talk about your lifelines.

Variations

- Individuals may want merely to look at each other's lifelines rather than talk about or explain them.
- Plenary/debrief based on questions such as: 'Were there any surprises?' 'Was there important learning in this for you?'

Materials

A large sheet of paper or flipchart paper and a copy of 'Reflecting on Your Distinctive Pattern of Experience' for each participant. A range of coloured pens/pencils for the students to use in drawing their lifelines.

Source: This exercise has been adapted from various workshops attended and also from Hopson and Scally (1984).

Reflecting on your Distinctive Pattern of Experience: Handout

1 What does my graph suggest about my *priorities* in life?

2 Does anything in my graph surprise me?

3 In what ways are the success and fulfilment lines associated?

4 How important has 'success' been in my life up to now? Why? How important is it right now? Why?

5 *What specific school/college/work activities or relationships* have brought me most fulfilment, joy and satisfaction? Why?

6 Focusing on the turning points on the fulfilment line:

   - What do the *peaks* have in common?
   - What do the *troughs* have in common?
   - What do the *slopes* and *plateaux* have in common?

7 Focusing on the turning points on the success line:

   - What do the *peaks* have in common?
   - What do the *troughs* have in common?
   - What do the *slopes* and *plateaux* have in common?

8 What kinds of *risks* have I taken? What has been the impulse behind each one? Do these risks turn out mostly positively or negatively for me?

9 Did I have to take these risks or did I have a choice?

10 What sorts of incidents became crises for me? Did I miss any of the challenges that they posed? If I did, what lessons may this offer to guide me in the future?

LETTER TO YOURSELF

Aim

To help the student to clarify what they want to get out of the first year of the course.

Procedure

1 Ask students to consider in pairs the question, 'What do I want to get out of this course in addition to passing the examinations?'
2 Brainstorm answers to the same question.
3 Tell the students that that is the end of the group activity part of the exercise apart from a general open discussion session at the end. For the rest of the session they will be working alone. Ask each student to note down any of the goals that have emerged that apply to them personally. This includes anything that came up when they were working in pairs, or anything from the brainstorm or anything that they haven't yet mentioned.
4 Ask the students to use their notes to write a letter to themselves in response to the question, 'What do I want to get out of this course in addition to passing the examinations?' Remind them to sign their letter.
5 Give them envelopes and ask them to write their names on the front and then to seal their letters inside.
6 Ask them to consider a good time to open their letter to see how they are doing. Then ask them to write that date on the envelope and then to put the letter away and not to open it until the date.
7 Plenary discussion.

GOALS FOR THE COURSE

Aims

- To help students to clarify their goals for the course.
- To help students to discover the impediments to realizing their goals and the actions that they can take to remove the impediments.

Procedure

1 Ask students to consider in pairs the question, 'What do I want to get out of this course in addition to passing the examinations?'
2 Brainstorm answers to the same question.
3 Tell the students that that is the end of the group activity part of the exercise apart from a general open discussion session at the end. For the rest of the session they will be working alone. Ask each student to write down any of the goals that have emerged that apply to them personally. This includes anything that came up when they were working in pairs, or anything from the brainstorm or anything that they haven't yet mentioned.
4 Distribute several copies of the 'setting goals' sheet. Ask the students to write each of their goals on a separate sheet in the space provided. Then ask them to complete the sheet for each of the goals that they have listed.
5 Plenary – a general open discussion on the usefulness of this exercise.

Source: University of Nottingham M Ed (Human Relations) course.

Setting Goals: Handout

I want to achieve the following goal:

What could keep me from achieving this goal?

( ) I don't have the skills, ability and/or knowledge.
( ) I don't want it badly enough to really work for it.
( ) I'm afraid that I might fail.
( ) I'm afraid of what others might think.
( ) Others don't want me to reach this goal.
( ) The goal is really too difficult ever to accomplish.

Any other reasons?

What are some of the things that I could do so that the above don't prevent me from reaching my goal?

Who could help me?

Name(s):   Kind of help:

What good things might happen if I reach this goal?

What bad things might happen if I reach this goal?

Do I still want to reach this goal?   ( )   Yes
                                                             ( )   No

What are the first steps that I could take to reach this goal?

What else must I do if I am really to succeed?

Am I going to take the above steps?   ( )   Yes
                                                             ( )   No

Self-contract

I .... have decided to try to achieve the goal of

The first step I will take to reach this goal will be to

My target date for taking this first step is:

Date .... Signed ....

8 Some Activities for Returning Students

Experience . . . is not what happens to you, it's what you do with what happens to you. (Jaques 1985)

REASONS FOR A GOOD EXPERIENCE

Aim

To help returning students discover what they can do to improve their experience of higher education.

Procedure

1 Ask the students how they would rate their experience of higher education last year. Ask them to give a subjective score from 1 to 10 where 1 is 'terrible' and 10 is 'brilliant'.
2 Have a class discussion of possible reasons for students on the same course having very different quality experiences of it.
3 Ask four or five of the students who gave high scores to act as a 'panel of experts' in 'getting the most out of the course' to answer questions from the rest of the class.

RETURNING TO STUDY AFTER A PERIOD OF WORK PLACEMENT

Aims

- To acknowledge the 'restart' of the course and signify moving forward to a further stage.
- To reintegrate the students into a cohesive group.
- To clear out of the way any unfinished business from earlier parts of the course.

Procedure

1 Ask the students to *individually* compile a list headed 'Things about my placement that were good'. Then ask them to write another list of 'Things about my placement that were bad'. (Ten minutes)

2 Ask the students to find a partner and explain their lists to their neighbours. (Ten minutes)

3 Each pair finds another pair to form a group of four. In these new groups of four each student gets ten minutes to explain her placement including the type of work that she did and answer any questions about it. (40 minutes)

4 Conclude the session with a round of 'The most important thing that I got from my placement was . . .'

APPRAISAL INTERVIEW

Aim

- To help the students to reflect on what has worked for them on the course so far.
- To help them to develop goals for the forthcoming year and to consider ways of achieving their goals.

Procedure

1 Write the following questions large on a flipchart so that all the students can see them:

- What did you do well (academically or otherwise) last year?
- What have you found most rewarding about the course so far?
- What have you found most difficult?
- What would you like to do better?
- How/what/when/where would you like to develop? (If it would be helpful, divide this into long-term and short-term perspectives.)
- What resources/skills do you have that are currently being underutilized?
- What would an action plan for your future development include?

2 Ask students to form pairs – an A and a B. A uses the above questions as the basis of an appraisal interview with B for

about 20 minutes. Suggest that A takes notes if this would be helpful.

3 B then reciprocates (ie, conducts an appraisal interview with A for about 20 minutes).

4 Plenary. Discussion of the results of each of the questions. Suggest that students speak for themselves rather than for their partner (ie share what the results were when they were the interview*ee* rather than what they found out as the interviewer).

SELF-ESTEEM EXERCISE

Aims

- To help students become more aware of when they are being successful.
- To widen their range of options for the new year.

Procedure

1 Ask students to write down one thing that they did successfully in their previous year on the course that was not assessed (ie excluding coursework and examinations). Suggest that this need not be academic.

2 Ask them to call out their success while the tutor writes it on the board.

3 Ask students to copy down any of the things contributed by others that also apply to themselves and allow time for them to do this.

4 Plenary.

COURSE-MONITORING REPORTS

Aims

- To help students become more aware of the environment in which they are working.
- To enable the students to take more responsibility for their experience of the course.

Procedure

1 Divide the students into small groups.
2 Distribute copies of last year's course-monitoring report (and for earlier years?).
3 Ask the students to identify the major strengths and weaknesses that they would want to include if they were to produce their own course-monitoring report.
4 Ask the students to identify which of the problems that they have identified from the last year could possibly occur again this year.
5 Take each of the identified potential problem areas and brainstorm what actions or attitudes the *students* can take to resolve the problem or minimize its adverse consequences for them.

Materials

Copies of last year's course-monitoring reports (and earlier ones if appropriate).

REQUESTING FEEDBACK EXERCISE

Aims

- To enable the students to become more aware of how their behaviour within groups is perceived.
- To help the students to become more aware of the contribution of feedback to significant learning.

Procedure

1 Ask the group to sit in a circle.
2 Initiate a discussion of the value of feedback in learning and the difficulties that most of us have in giving others positive and negative feedback.
3 Inform the group members that this is an opportunity for anyone to seek information from those present about the way that other group members have experienced his or her behaviour. Display the list in the handout on a flipchart or distribute it to the students.
4 Stress the importance of the following three rules (which should also be on the flipchart or handout):

- *Participation is voluntary. No member of the group shall be compelled to either seek or give information.*
- *The information given shall be limited to what a person asks for.*
- *Observations should be substantiated by specifics of what has been said or done.*

5 Invite members of the group to seek feedback by asking for it along the following lines: 'I would like to know how you see me in relation to number 8.'

Variations

Invite the group members to give feedback by reference to the following scale:

5: Strongly agree
4: Agree
3: Unsure/don't know
2: Disagree
1: Strongly disagree

Source: Adapted from Smith (1983).

Requesting Feedback: Handout

1 Expresses self clearly and concisely.

2 Encourages group to keep to the job.

3 Takes the lead in initiating topics, concerns or procedures.

4 Offers constructive ideas as needed.

5 Contribute without cutting others off.

6 Helps get to the meat of issues.

7 Listens attentively to what others say.

8 Helps others express their ideas and learn.

9 Helps others feel at ease and is supportive.

10 Sticks too long to his or her point.

11 Avoids facing problems.

12 Seeks to impose his or her will on the group.

13 Sometimes gets defensive.

14 Is better at offering advice rather than support.

15 Tends to make comments that are judgmental or critical of the contributions of others.

- *Participation is voluntary. No member of the group is required to either seek or give information.*
- *The information given shall be limited to what a person asks for.*
- *Try to substantiate by facts, by specifics of what has been said or done.*

HELPING OTHERS IN TRANSITION

Aims

- To enable the students to help one another with their own transitions.
- To provide an opportunity to acquire additional strategies for coping with future life transitions.

Procedure

1 Ask the students to remember when they started the course.
2 Individuals are asked to write down anything that they remember about that time. Any thoughts? Any feelings? Anything that they enjoyed? Any people who helped? Any impressions? Anything funny that happened?
3 Then ask each person to think and write down who or what would have made it easier to fit into the new situation.
4 After sufficient time has been allowed for doing this, the whole group is asked to brainstorm, 'What we remember' and 'What would have helped?'
5 The group's attention is then turned to the fact that another group of new students has arrived to experience the same transition.
6 The large group can now be divided into small groups (or remain as one group), to work on the next stage of the task.
7 Each group is asked to identify what kind of help would be most appreciated by a new first-year student at each stage in the transition into higher education (eg, during the first week, the second week, etc).
8 The ideas generated by the groups can then be integrated and discussed. In particular, the students can be invited to discuss anything that they have learned that will help their own re-entry and anything that will help their own transitions in the future.
9 The group can then summarize its findings into its own 'Tips for Transitions' list, (eg find out as much as you can beforehand, make contact or talk to others who know, find people who can help and so on).

Variations

- The small groups are asked to prepare a plan or programme which would ensure a smooth transition for newcomers to the institution.

- The small groups are asked to produce a list of similarities and differences between school and higher education for the first-year students.
- The small groups are asked to produce a list of tips for new first-year students.
- Individuals could be asked to take responsibility for welcoming and getting to know two or three newcomers during the first week.

Source: Adapted from Hopson and Scally (1980).

SELF-ADVICE BRAINSTORM

Aim

To help returning students to reflect upon what they can do to get the most out their new year at college.

Procedure

1 Find the square root of the number in the class. On the basis of this prepare numbers A1, A2, A3 and so on; B1, B2, B3 and so on where the length of each series is equal (approximately) to the square root of the number in the class.

2 Distribute the numbers and form groups comprising all As, all Bs etc. Ask all of the groups to consider the following question: 'What advice would be helpful to first-year students on how to get the most out of their first year?'

3 After about ten minutes, reform the groups on the basis of each person's number (all the 1s, all the 2s etc). The group members report back what was achieved in their first group.

4 After about ten minutes, go round the groups in a 'round robin' fashion (ie one piece of advice per group) and record the results on a flipchart or chalkboard. Continue until all the advice that was generated in the groups has been recorded.

5 Plenary discussion focused on the question, 'Which pieces of your advice are also applicable to yourselves as second – (or third) – year students?'

Materials

Flipcharts, marker pens and bluetack.

GOALS AND ACTIONS

(This exercise could also be used with new students).

Aims

- To develop a positive climate and a spirit of cooperation among those who will be working together.
- To foster teamwork within group activity.

Procedure

1 Divide the group into teams of about four to six (possibly on the basis of seminar groups).
2 Ask the group to spend the first ten minutes developing a collective mental image (verbalized) of what their working situation would preferably be like a term from now. (Eg 'What could it potentially become from a positive viewpoint?')
3 Ask each team to develop a skeletal action plan listing the items directly or indirectly under their control that must be accomplished in the next term to achieve the overall image.
4 Ask each team to present a brief report to the total group.

Possible discussion questions

- How feasible is your overall plan?
- What factors might prevent you from being successful? (Lack of agreement on the goal or plan; lack of resources; unforeseen events.)
- How often will you review your progress toward the goal?

Materials

Flipcharts, marker pens and bluetack.

Source: Adapted from Newstrom and Scannell (1980).

9 Getting Feedback from the Students

If you haven't made any mistakes lately, you must be doing something wrong. (Jeffers 1987)

FEEDBACK (1):
Graffiti Feedback Board

Aim

To provide an anonymous outlet for ongoing student reactions during the induction programme.

Procedure

1 Course evaluation usually occurs at the end of a programme. The incentive to treat the results seriously is reduced by the fact that changes will occur too late to affect the students providing the feedback.
2 An alternative (or a supplement) is to use graffiti boards. A graffiti board is a poster board, flipchart, or chalkboard on which students can express (ventilate) their observations, reactions, ideas or emotions to the tutors or the rest of the group. This can be done on an anonymous basis if the students choose. Topics can be provided at the top ('course content', 'physical facilities' etc) or the feedback may be solicited on a totally unstructured basis.

Possible discussion questions

- How many of you agree with the comment made about . . . ?
- What's the basis for the comment about . . . ?
- What corrective steps can we take *now* to change the situation?

Materials

Flipchart or similar medium on which to write.

Source: Newstrom and Scannell (1980).

FEEDBACK (2):
Sample Feedback Forms

Aims

- To provide early feedback on each day's activities.
- To review the learning from the day's activities.

Procedure

1 Produce a very simple feedback form for the students to complete and return at the end of each day. This might include, for example, only:

- How useful did you find today's session?
  - ( ) 5 Very useful
  - ( ) 4 Quite useful
  - ( ) 3 Unsure/don't know
  - ( ) 2 Not very useful
  - ( ) 1 No use at all
- What was the best thing about today's session for you?
- What was the least useful thing about today's session?
- Any suggestions for improving today's session?

2 Distribute and collect the (anonymous) forms during the last ten minutes of *each* day's session. Tabulate the responses to the first question and prepare a brief impressionistic analysis of the other questions. Share the results at the beginning of the next day's session. Use this presentation as the basis of a summary review, clarification of misperceptions, and as a foundation for introducing the new day's topics.

Possible discussion questions

- What did we do yesterday that contributed most to your learning experience?

- How did the group's consensus of the most useful and least useful things about yesterday differ from your own?

Materials

Enough simple feedback forms for the whole class.

Source: Adapted from Newstrom and Scannell (1980).

FEEDBACK (3):
Nominal Group Technique

Aims

- To prepare the students for participating in course development and providing feedback to staff by introducing them to this method of student evaluation of courses.
- To obtain feedback on the induction programme.

Procedure

1 Spend a few minutes introducing the nominal group technique and explaining why we are using this approach. Then distribute the 'notes for students' (or project it as an OHP slide) and check that they understand what they have to do.
2 Ask the students to spend a few minutes *individually* writing down 3–5 brief comments about aspects of the induction programme. Ask them to consider including compliments as well as criticisms.
3 Divide the students into *groups* of 12 to 16 (use tutorial groups?). Give each group flipchart paper, bluetack and a marker pen. Then ask each group to form a single composite list of about 15 comments that they feel are most important and record these on the flipchart paper. This can easily be done by sharing the comments in a 'round robin' fashion (one response per person each time).

- They do not have to reach a consensus on these. For example, if there is disagreement, two contradictory comments can be included on the list.
- Criticism of the comments of others is discouraged but *clarification* in reponse to questions is encouraged.

4 Each person then evaluates the comments on the group list and individually 'votes' for them, giving 5 for the most important, 4 for the next most important and so on.

5 'Votes' for each comment are then collected within the group and converted to figures for the percentage of the maximum (if all the members of a group gave 5 to a comment it would get 100%). A group report is prepared showing the comments receiving the highest scores on a copy of the attached report form and given to you as the tutor.

Materials

Flipchart paper, bluetack and marker pens.

Feedback (3)
Nominal Group Technique: Handout

Notes for Students

Individually, spend a few minutes writing down about 3–5 brief comments about aspects of the induction programme. Consider including compliments as well as criticisms.

In groups, form a single composite list of about 15 comments that you feel are most important and record these on the flipchart paper (or chalkboard). This can easily be done by sharing the comments in a 'round robin' fashion (one response per person each time).

- You do not have to reach a consensus on comments. For example, if there is disagreement, two contradictory comments can be included on the list.

- Criticism of the comments of others is discouraged but clarification in response to questions is encouraged.

Individually, evaluate the comments on the group list and 'vote' for them by giving 5 for the most important, 4 for the next most important and so on.

In groups:

(a) collect in 'votes' for each item, add them and note them in the 'raw score' column on the sheet provided.

(b) convert the 'raw score' for each item to a figure for 'percentage of maximum'. With n students in a group the maximum raw score that a comment can get is $5 \times n$. So to convert a raw score to a 'percentage of maximum', simply multiply each raw score by $100/(5 \times n)$.

Finally, hand in your group report to your tutor.

Feedback (3) Nominal Group Technique: Course Evaluation – Group Report

Number of students in group:

Comments	Raw Score	% of max
1		
2		
3		
4		
5		
6		
7		
8		

Comments	Raw Score	% of max
9		
10		
11		
12		
13		
14		
15		

10   A Few Other Ideas

Life is if nothing else a persistent teacher. It will repeat a lesson over and over (and over and over) until it is learned. . . . The good news is that we learn all we need to know eventually. The bad news: the lessons continue until they are learned. (McWilliams, J-R and McWilliams, P 1990)

Miscellaneous idea 1: Personal journal

Suggest that students keep a *personal* journal of what happens to them during their first crucial week of college.
You could suggest that the students might include the following:

- useful information
- reflections
- insights
- ideas
- resolutions

Alternatively, you could get the class to brainstorm what they think it would be useful to include in their journals. (You might also consider setting aside an hour at the end of each day for them to write up their journals if they choose to do so.)

Miscellaneous idea 2: Glossary

Ask the students to produce a glossary of terms, concepts and the like that emerge during the induction programme.
Alternatively, produce a list of terms and concepts that you think it would be good if they understood. Here are a few examples:

- intellectual rigour
- use of the critical faculties
- transferable skills in higher education
- positive feedback

- negative feedback
- seminar
- lecture
- 'active' learning

Miscellaneous idea 3: Homework

Homework can be used to facilitate reflection upon what has happened during the day and for preparation for the activities of the next day. A little voluntary sharing of the results could be a useful way of starting the new day. Here are a few possible 'homework' questions that you could ask:

- Write down (a) the most important things that you *learned* today and (b) any *actions* that it would be useful to take in the light of what you have learned.
- Write down positive and negative feelings that you have about your transition into higher education.
- What is involved in making a successful transition into higher education?
- What resources are available to you to help you to cope with, and make the most of, your transition into higher education?
- What does it mean to be a 'successful' student?
- In what ways would you expect to be different at the end of the course that you are just starting than you are now? (In what ways are you different from how you were n years ago – where n is the length of the course in years?)
- Write down five qualities that you have that will help you to succeed on this course.
- Success is often a matter of finding the right attitude. Write down what you consider to be the three most important attitudes to help a new student succeed on his or her course of higher education.
- What are the differences between . . .

  - school and college?
  - a school teacher and a college lecturer?
  - a school pupil and a student in higher education?
  - criticism and feedback?
  - you as you are now and you as you hope to be at the end of the course?
  - active and passive learning?

- And some 'homework' questions for returning students:

  - How different does it feel to be starting again this year compared to when you first started the course?
  - What have you learned about yourself from last year?
  - What are you going to do differently this year from what you did last year?
  - What has proved to be more difficult than you expected when you started the course?
  - What did you hope to do as a student when you started the course that you haven't yet done?
  - What will you have regrets about if you don't get to do this year?

Miscellaneous idea 4: Add your own ideas

We've left this space empty for you to write down your own ideas for induction activities.

Index of Induction Activities

- To encourage individuals to share positive qualities with others.

COOPERATIVE GAME   39

- To develop cooperation and trust.
- To have some fun.

INFORMATION NEEDS   41

- To identify information that the students want about the course, department or institution.

3: Acquiring Relevant Information

SWAP SHOP   42

- To obtain new ideas and information.
- To encourage group participation.

TREASURE HUNT   43

- To discover information about the course, department, institution or town that will be useful in the student's transition to higher education.
- To engage course members in a task-orientated activity so they can begin developing a team identity and cohesiveness.

STUDENT INTERVIEWS   44

- To familiarize students with staff and their expectations and attitudes about the course.
- To find out information about the course department.

COURSE HANDBOOK   45

- To familiarize students with the information contained within the course handbook.
- To engage the students in a syndicate-type activity to facilitate group identity and cohesiveness.

QUIZ   46

- To familiarize the students with information about the course, department, institution or town.

THE STUDENT AS EXPERT   47

- To familiarize the students with information about the course, department, institution or town.

- To help students to become aware of each other as learning resources.
- To raise self-confidence and self-esteem of students by enabling each to acquire special expertise in an area.

4: Coping with the Problems of Transition into Higher Education

- To clear out of the way any unfinished business from earlier parts of the course.

APPRAISAL INTERVIEW   118

- To help the students to reflect on what has worked for them on the course so far.
- To help them to develop goals for the forthcoming year and to consider ways of achieving their goals.

SELF-ESTEEM EXERCISE   119

- To help students become more aware of when they are being successful.
- To widen their range of options for the new year.

COURSE-MONITORING REPORTS   119

- To help students become more aware of the environment in which they are working.
- To enable the students to take more responsibility for their experience of the course.

REQUESTING FEEDBACK EXERCISE   120

- To enable the students to become more aware of how their behaviour within groups is perceived.
- To help the students to become more aware of the contribution of feedback to significant learning.

HELPING OTHERS IN TRANSITION   123

- To enable the students to help one another with their own transitions.
- To provide an opportunity to acquire additional strategies for coping with future life transitions.

SELF-ADVICE BRAINSTORM   124

- To help returning students to reflect upon what they can do to get the most out of their new year at college.

GOALS AND ACTIONS   125

- To develop a positive climate and a spirit of cooperation among those who will be working together.
- To foster teamwork within group activity.

9: Getting Feedback from the Student

10: A Few Other Ideas

References

Brandes and Ginnis (1986) *A Guide to Student-centred Learning* Blackwell, Oxford.

Brandes, D and Phillips, H (1978) *Gamesters' Handbook Vol 1* Hutchinson, London.

Gibbs, G (1981) *Teaching Students to Learn: A Student-centred Approach* Open University Press, Milton Keynes.

Gibbs, G and Jaques, D (1987) *147 Ideas for Non-traditional Teaching* Oxford Polytechnic Educational Methods Unit, Oxford.

Habeshaw, T, Habeshaw, S and Gibbs, G (1987) *53 Interesting Ways of Helping Your Students to Study* Technical and Educational Services Ltd, Bristol.

Holmes, T H and Rae, R H (1967) The social readjustment rating scale, *Journal of Psychosomatic Research* 11, 213–18.

Hopson, B and Scally, M (1980) *Lifeskills Teaching Programme No. 1* Lifeskills Associates, Leeds.

Hopson, B and Scally, M (1984) *Build Your Own Rainbow: A Workbook for Career and Life Management* Lifeskills Associates, Leeds.

Jaques, D (1985) *Learning in Groups* Croom Helm, Beckenham.

Jeffers, S (1987) *Feel the Fear and Do It Anyway* Century, London.

McWilliams, J-R and McWilliams, P (1990) *Life 101* Prelude Press, Los Angeles.

Newstrom, J and Scannell, E (1980) *Games Trainers Play* McGraw Hill, New York.

Parkes, C (1975) *Bereavement: Studies of Grief in Adult Life* Penguin, Harmondsworth.

Parlett, M and Simons, H (1976) *Up to Expectations: A Study of the Student's First Few Weeks of Higher Education* Nuffield Foundation, London.

Pfeiffer, J W and Jones, J E (eds) (1973) *A Handbook of Structured Experiences for Human Relations Training* University Associates, La Jolla, California.

Raaheim, K and Wankowski, J (1981) *Helping Students to Learn at University.*

Sheehy, G (1977) Pathfinders Bantam Books, New York.

Smith, R M (1983) *Learning How to Learn: Applied Theory for Adults* Open University Press, Milton Keynes.

Wallechinsky, D et al (1977) *The Book of Lists* William Morris Inc, New York.